CONSTRUCTION:
BUILDING
THE
IMPOSSIBLE

In this photograph of October 4, 1909, workers and wrecking cranes struggle to free a steam shovel from one of the many mudslides that slowed construction of the Panama Canal.

INNOVATORS

CONSTRUCTION:
BUILDING
THE
IMPOSSIBLE

Nathan Aaseng

The Oliver Press, Inc.
Minneapolis

The Oliver Press, Inc.
Charlotte Square
5707 West 36th Street
Minneapolis, MN 55416-2510

Library of Congress Cataloging-in-Publication Data
Aaseng, Nathan.
Construction : building the impossible / Nathan Aaseng
p. cm. — (Innovators)
Includes bibliographical references and index.
    Summary: Profiles eight builders and their famous construction
projects, including Imhotep and the Step Pyramid, Alexandre Eiffel
and the Eiffel Tower, and William Lamb and the Empire State
Building.
ISBN 1-881508-59-5 (library binding)
1. Civil engineering—History—Juvenile literature. 2. Civil engineers—Biography—Juvenile Literature. [1. Civil engineering.
2. Building. 3. Buildings. 4. Civil engineers.] I. Title. II. Series.
TA149 .A27 2000
624'.092'2—dc21

                                    98-51815
                                       CIP
                                       AC

ISBN 1-881508-59-5
Printed in the United States of America
06 05 04 03 02 01 00   8 7 6 5 4 3 2 1

CONTENTS

Reconstructing the Great Builders

Although the seven structures described in this book are renowned the world over, most of the innovators behind them are largely unknown. This book attempts to shine the light of recognition on the creators of some of the most awe-inspiring construction projects of all time.

Singling out the geniuses behind the human-made wonders of the world is often an impossible task because some of the great builders of the past are unknown to us. The breathtaking Taj Mahal in Agra, India, is an example. Shah Jahan, emperor of India from 1628 to 1658, ordered the mausoleum built to honor his wife, Mumtaz Mahal, who died in childbirth in 1630. Combining size and exquisite beauty, it continues to rank today as one of the architectural wonders of the world.

We know the Taj Mahal attracted the most skilled artisans of the time and that 20,000 laborers worked for at least 20 years to complete it. Yet who

mausoleum: a large stately building housing one or several burial vaults

Historians know who ordered the Taj Mahal built and when and why. But the architect who designed it remains anonymous.

An **architect** designs and supervises the construction of buildings and other structures.

designed and supervised the construction of this grand monument of love?

Legend claims a Turkish architect, Ustad Isa, himself a grieving widower, presented the winning design to the emperor. Shah Jahan, the tale continues, was so pleased with the structure that when it was completed, he beheaded Ustad Isa to prevent him from ever building anything more beautiful. There is, however, no evidence that Ustad Isa ever existed.

Perhaps Ahmad, a Persian engineer who directed other architectural projects for Shah Jahan, is the man behind the building. Another engineer, Ali Mardan Khan, is recorded as the designer of the Taj Mahal's dome. But it is also written that he arrived in Agra in 1638, six years after construction began, so he probably was not responsible for the overall design. The identity of that architect (or architects) will remain a mystery.

An equally frustrating problem for those who wish to give the great builders their due is that because complex engineering projects often required so many brilliant and skilled planners, we cannot assign credit to one individual. In terms of the number of workers, the length of the construction period, and the size of the finished product, the Great Wall of China ranks as the world's greatest construction project. At one time, the wall wound for several thousand miles over the ridges and valleys of China. Even today, more than 2,200 years after the wall was begun, about 1,500 miles (2,400 kilometers) remain.

Who is responsible for designing and building the Great Wall? We know that the project began

in the third century B.C. because Emperor Qin Shi Huangdi wanted to prevent the bands of nomads who lived to the north from looting or conquering China. General Meng Tian supervised this first stage of construction, and he is praised for his ingenious use of natural barriers. But over the centuries, many rulers and architects altered, added to, or rebuilt the wall.

This protection strategy was generally successful. Impressive as it must have been, however, the wall did not always achieve its purpose. Mongol

In China, mountains symbolize peaceful dragons. Many thought of the Great Wall as the dragon's spine.

invaders, united by the fierce leader Genghis Khan, swept past the barrier to overrun China. His grandson Kublai Khan deposed the Chinese emperor in 1279 and began his own Yuan dynasty. When the Chinese finally threw out the Mongol rulers about 100 years later, the new Ming dynasty made an even more bold attempt to build an unbroken line of defense across the northern border of their country.

Using earth, stone, wood, and bricks, the Chinese constructed a wall averaging 23 feet (7 meters) high, 22 feet (6.7 meters) wide at the base, and 16 feet (4.9 meters) wide at the top. In 1644, they finally completed a wall that stretched 4,000 miles (6,440 kilometers) and included forts and towers built into the wall at key defensive points. The Great Wall of China is not the result of any one person's inspiration or planning, but evolved over a period of more than 1,800 years.

Like the Great Wall, most of today's spectacular engineering and construction achievements are too enormous to credit to any individual. The greatest tunnels and largest domes in existence today were the combined work of a great many talented people.

This book focuses on some of the individuals whose creative genius or organizational skill helped bring about some of the engineering wonders of the world. The first true pyramid, the Step Pyramid, can be traced to one Egyptian master builder, Imhotep (born about 2700 B.C.), whose innovation—building with stone—seems so obvious now.

A shipworm inspired French engineer Marc Brunel to design a shield that held back the earth while he began tunneling under the Thames River in London in 1825. New York's Brooklyn Bridge was designed by John Roebling, an engineer and steel cable manufacturer. His son, Washington, completed the steel pathway over the East River despite overwhelming personal and engineering problems.

Alexandre Gustave Eiffel was both a meticulous engineer and planner. These skills enabled him in just two years to construct in the center of Paris what was then the tallest structure in the world, the Eiffel Tower. Army engineer George W. Goethals commanded a civilian work force numbering 45,000 that carved a canal through the mountains and jungle of Panama. This waterway connected the Atlantic and Pacific Oceans.

Like Goethals, engineer Frank Crowe also literally moved a river and mountains to build the Hoover Dam. The dam would supply water and electric power to the growing population in the western United States. Architect William Lamb won the race to erect the tallest skyscraper in New York City when he finished the magnificent Empire State Building in 1931.

None of these engineers and designers operated without a great deal of expert assistance from trained supervisors and an army of contractors and laborers. Moreover, their projects could never have been realized without major financial backing and a good deal of political maneuvering. Yet each stands out for his unique contribution to an awe-inspiring feat of technology that has had a profound impact on society.

High above the East River, riggers lash together the steel cables that suspend the floor of the Brooklyn Bridge.

Colonel George W. Goethals supervised construction of the Panama Canal for seven years.

CHAPTER ONE

Imhotep and the Step Pyramid

We often think of engineering as a profession belonging to the industrialized world. Engineers employ the powerful machines of technology to create marvels of the modern age such as buildings, highways, and bridges. They design their creations using complex mathematical formulas, many of which require calculators and computers.

Yet one of the most famous and important engineers of all time lived about 4,700 years ago. With no machinery at his disposal, simple mathematics, and precious few tools of any kind, this engineer oversaw the creation of a breathtaking monument that still stands today. More importantly, he pioneered a simple concept that entirely changed the way people constructed buildings.

History has recorded few names of those who designed and supervised the construction of the great structures of the ancient world. In fact, other than the occasional king or military leader, individuals

The Step Pyramid in Egypt still stands almost 5,000 years after it was erected because the builder, Imhotep (c. 2700 b.c.), used a new building material— stone.

who lived at that time are mostly unknown. One exception, however, is Imhotep, the Egyptian master builder who was responsible for building the Step Pyramid, the forerunner of the Great Pyramids.

Few details of Imhotep's personal life have survived. But evidence exists that he was born sometime around 2700 B.C. Although his birthplace is not known, Imhotep lived a good deal of his life in the village of Gebelein, south of the city of Luxor. He was the son of Ka-nefer, a skilled builder who served in the Egyptian government.

Imhotep far exceeded his father's skill as a master builder. He became the personal favorite building consultant of Djoser (spelled Zoser by some historians), who ruled the ancient kingdom of Egypt during the 2600s B.C. Imhotep performed his tasks so well that Djoser installed him in the highest religious position in the land, and, at one point, made

A depiction of Egypt's King Djoser surrounded by hieroglyphics, the Egyptian form of writing

him second in command over all of Egypt. Both were rare honors for someone not of royal blood.

As Imhotep's reputation grew, stories and legends about him spread throughout Egypt and into other countries. One popular story explained both his position of power and his status as a religious figure. Apparently, the Nile River failed to flood for several years in a row during Djoser's reign. This was disastrous because the Nile carried rich soil from thousands of miles of African river valleys north through Egypt to the Mediterranean Sea. When the river flooded, this soil was deposited along the farmlands of the upper Nile. Farmers in Egypt needed these floods to provide nutrients and water for their crops. When the floodwaters failed to come year after year, the crops withered.

After the seventh consecutive year without flooding, Egypt faced a terrible famine. In desperation, Djoser turned to Imhotep for advice. Imhotep replied that Djoser could solve the problem by gaining the favor of Khnur, one of the gods of creation. Immediately, Djoser presented gifts to Khnur at one of the god's temples. According to legend, the Nile promptly rose and overflowed its banks. The crops grew again, and the Egyptians were fed.

The widely talented Imhotep also won praise as a wise man, a great writer, and a magician. During his life, Egyptians honored him with a wide variety of titles including Chancellor, High Priest, Vizier, and First One under the King. Hundreds of years after his death, Egyptians still worshiped Imhotep as the son of the god Ptah, god of artists and craftsmen.

Imhotep's fame spread to Greece, but the Greeks were more impressed with Imhotep's knowledge of medicine. They built temples in Imhotep's honor that attracted crowds of sick and injured people hoping to be healed.

THE BREAKTHROUGH

Imhotep's greatest challenge involved the building of a burial chamber for Djoser. Burial was an extremely important rite to the Egyptians. Because they believed that the deceased would be transported to a new world, the body had to be preserved as carefully as possible to be ready for that final journey. Supplies for this great voyage to the hereafter were uncertain, so Egyptians wanted to be buried with riches and the necessities of life to sustain them along the way. They even included boats in the burial vault as a means of transportation.

One of the unfortunate byproducts of this religious belief was an epidemic of grave robbing. All those riches lying unprotected in a burial vault proved an irresistible temptation to thieves.

Master designers such as Imhotep worked under two guidelines that were in almost direct conflict. First, the burial vault had to be secure so that the riches contained within could not be easily stolen. This could best be done by hiding the vault in a place where thieves would not think to look. But secondly, the burial place had to be a monument that showed off the might and power of the ruler. Unfortunately, any memorial so elaborate and majestic that it overwhelmed the observer was also a giant advertisement for where the body and the treasures were buried. Builders tried to solve this problem by hiding the burial vaults deep within these elaborate monuments and constructing false tunnels and doors.

The Egyptian rulers set aside a section of land, known as a necropolis, or city of the dead, for their burial tombs. Djoser's tomb was to be built in a necropolis called Saqqara (or Sakkara) in the desert southwest of Memphis, the capital of Djoser's kingdom. This was about 15 miles (24 kilometers) from the center of the present Egyptian capital of Cairo.

Imhotep had proven himself so gifted an architect and builder that Djoser gave him the freedom to design the burial vault. Imhotep began by selecting a piece of land on a high plateau overlooking Memphis so that the burial monument would be visible to those in the capital city.

Had Imhotep been a traditional builder, he would have produced a structure similar to the other tombs that had been built at Saqqara in the previous 500 years. These were all in the form of a mastaba. A mastaba was a large, low-built rectangle resembling a large shoe box. Like virtually all buildings in Egypt, a mastaba was constructed with bricks made of mud and straw. The burial chamber was dug deep into the ground beneath the mastaba and was surrounded by many other chambers and storerooms.

Imhotep originally planned to use the traditional form of the mastaba for Djoser. To satisfy the ruler's desire for a grand monument that the people of the world would hold in awe long after Djoser's death, Imhotep wanted to design a mastaba larger and more elaborate than any previous ones. While pondering ways in which he could surpass all other mastabas, an inspiration struck him. Ancient Egyptian historian Manetho, writing 2,400 years

necropolis: a large and elaborate cemetery. From the Greek words *necro*, which means dead body or corpse, and *polis*, which means city.

later, summed up Imhotep's innovative contribution to the building profession: "This man also discovered the art of building with hewn stones."

To those who have grown up among stone buildings, this might seem a rather obvious discovery. But prior to Imhotep, no one thought of stone as a building material except for use as flooring and an occasional ornament. Stone is difficult to work with. It is hard, extremely heavy, and can be shaped only with great difficulty. In contrast, mud bricks can easily be molded to the exact size and form desired. (Wood is also a versatile building material, but it was not widely available in the desert climate of Egypt. Small wonder that the Egyptians built with mud bricks.)

Some historians have concluded that it was Imhotep's quest for a majestic structure that led him to experiment with stone. Perhaps Imhotep imagined a structure that would stand forever as an eternal reminder of Djoser's might and glory. Bricks easily chipped and crumbled, but the great stones of the earth seemed indestructible. Why not, then, build the mastaba entirely out of this everlasting material?

With a grandiose vision of an eternal burial vault in his mind, Imhotep organized what historians have called the world's first great construction project. He began work sometime in the mid-2600s B.C. by sinking a central shaft 92 feet (28 meters) deep and 22 feet (6.7 meters) square at the bottom. The workers used a small wrecking ball made from a hard rock called dolerite to loosen the stone. Next they took chisels and other sharp-edged stonecutters made from copper or dolerite to dig the shaft.

Then Imhotep assembled several large work forces. One of these groups hauled limestone from a nearby quarry. Using logs and ropes, they pried the large chunks onto wooden sleds, which they then pulled to the building site. Imhotep planned to use local limestone for the core of the structure. But to

Most historians think that the Egyptians hauled the huge stones of the pyramids with only human labor, ropes, and perhaps ramps made of sand.

limestone: a sedimentary rock made up mostly of the mineral calcite. Often used as a building material and to process steel and chemicals.

make the mastaba more beautiful, he insisted on higher quality white limestone for the outside surfaces. This limestone could be found only at the cliff of Tura, located on the east bank of the Nile River. Imhotep sent workers to cut huge blocks of stone from this cliff. Another work force struggled to get the blocks onto boats and across the Nile. Others dragged the stones to the building site, where carvers shaped them into the desired form.

The genius of Imhotep was that he constantly sought and found new approaches to building. He was not afraid to experiment and to revise his plans when a new idea occurred to him. Not content with just using a new building material, Imhotep also toyed with the shape of the mastaba. Instead of the usual oblong shape, he tightened the rectangle into a square with each side 207 feet (63 meters) long and 26 feet (7.9 meters) high.

After viewing what he had created, however, Imhotep decided that even this wonderful mastaba was not glorious enough for his king. He had the base widened on each side, but that was still not majestic enough. He widened it some more. Imhotep's plans grew bolder as he sought to create the greatest building the world had ever seen.

Sometime during this process, Imhotep came up with yet another of what one historian called "one of those developments that afterward seem inevitable but that would have been impossible without an experimenting genius." Imhotep decided to place a smaller mastaba on top of the original. Next, an even smaller one was put on top of that, which was topped by another still smaller mastaba. The effect was similar to a giant flight of stairs. Some scholars suggest that Imhotep's intent was to create a ladder so that the dead ruler's soul could climb to the sky. Or he may have simply sought a way to raise up the monument to an imposing height.

At any rate, Imhotep began constructing the world's first free-standing stone monument. Never satisfied that he had succeeded in his goal of creating the ultimate memorial, he altered his design again. This time he added two more layers to the structure for a total of six. The result was what has come to be known as the Step Pyramid. At about 200 feet (60 meters) high, the pyramid towered over the other mastabas in the necropolis.

This pyramid, however, was only the centerpiece of an elaborate complex such as the world had never seen. How Imhotep managed to coordinate such a mammoth project is not recorded, but he surrounded his pyramid with replicas of the buildings of the royal palace complex in Memphis. The original structures were made of brick and wood, but Imhotep created the replicas out of stone. He then surrounded the complex with an enormous wall. Made of white limestone cut to the shape of small blocks of brick, the wall stood 32 feet (9.8 meters) high. It stretched for 1,690 feet (515 meters) on its longer sides and 860 feet (262 meters) on the short sides. To protect the pyramid from grave robbers, he built 13 false entrances to the complex and provided only 1 actual entrance.

Imhotep's efforts to thwart grave robbers failed. When the Step Pyramid was excavated by archaeologists in the 1800s, only a mummified foot was found in the king's vault.

THE RESULT

Imhotep came as close as anyone to creating an eternal monument. His Step Pyramid still stands, although much of the astonishing burial complex that surrounded it is now in ruins.

More important, however, is the influence Imhotep had on the development of his country. Once Imhotep produced his stunning burial complex, the proud kings who succeeded Djoser could not allow their builders to construct lesser structures for themselves. They took up Imhotep's innovation of building with stone, and Imhotep's massive, stepped tower became the pattern for all royal burial tombs that followed.

Not content with merely copying the burial site of the earlier ruler, Egyptian pharaohs went to astonishing lengths to outdo all previous kings with ever more spectacular death monuments. Building on Imhotep's ideas, they erected larger step towers. Then pharaohs constructed smooth-sided pyramids with a facing of stone instead of Imhotep's steps leading up to the sky. Eventually, Egyptian royalty constructed more than 70 huge pyramids. The common people, meanwhile, may have built many more lesser structures for their own burial use.

The race for prestige in burial vaults reached its peak with the largest of the three Great Pyramids of Giza, completed around 2600 B.C. This towering mountain of stone—the largest stone building ever constructed—honored the pharaoh Khufu (also known by his Greek name, Cheops). Made up of

This group of three pyramids at Giza, outside modern Cairo, are known as the Great Pyramids. Khufu (front) is the largest; the other two are Khafra (center) and Menkaura (rear). Considered one of the Seven Wonders of the Ancient World, the pyramids are the only surviving wonder.

The families of kings, called dynasties, ruled for 3,000 years and are grouped into the Old, Middle, and New Kingdoms. Most of the pyramids were constructed during the Old Kingdom, the third through sixth dynasties (about 2680 to 2180 B.C.).

almost 2.5 million stone blocks, Khufu originally rose 481 feet (146 meters) above the Egyptian sand and measured 756 feet (230 meters) on each side at its base. Time and shifting sands have reduced Khufu to its current height of 450 feet (137 meters).

The monument, which still stands today, is all the more impressive given the fact that those who built it had precious little equipment. They had to transport the stones, some of which weighed over 7 tons (6.4 metric tons), to the construction site without the help of wheels, let alone motors. Workers then had to find a way to pile these stones precisely on top of one another without a pulley. Some experts believe they hauled the stones up ramps.

The supervisors of the Great Pyramids followed Imhotep's lead in organizing massive teams of workers, each of whom was given a particular task. They had to construct a series of canals along the Nile to the construction site to transport the stone as well as food for as many as 100,000 workers.

Some historians believe the construction projects pioneered by Imhotep for the giant burial monuments were at least partially responsible for the rise of Egyptian civilization. The projects brought many thousands of people from different areas of the land together in an organized, government-sponsored effort. As a result of that endeavor, the provinces and tribes of people became more interconnected in a system that produced one of the most powerful ancient civilizations.

In a way, the Great Pyramids inspired by Imhotep's innovation provide the best tribute to his genius even though they dwarf Imhotep's Step Pyramid. Today, most people have seen pictures of the Great Pyramids, while relatively few know about the existence of the Step Pyramid. Yet despite the colossal size of the Khufu Pyramid, the architects and engineers of that project never made their way into the history books. That honor was reserved for Imhotep—the man who started the whole concept of stone-building and pyramid construction.

A view from Khufu (or Cheops), the largest of the Great Pyramids

CHAPTER TWO

Marc Brunel and the Thames Tunnel

In the early nineteenth century, the underground was a forbidden world entered only by a few brave miners and cave explorers. Clergy warned people to stay away from the nether regions—the home of evil forces. Fear of the underground kept many people from using the few tunnels that did exist. For example, a tunnel completed as part of France's San Quentin canal system in 1810 found no takers among the boat captains. Officials offered a lifetime of free tolls to any boat operator who would pass through the tunnel on opening day. Only one captain overcame his fear and took advantage of the generous offer.

Beyond the psychological aversion to tunnels, engineering problems prevented their widespread use. If the ground was solid rock, how could people blast through it? Dynamite would not be invented until 1866. If the ground was soft, how could workers keep it from caving in during the excavating?

Pedestrians descend the steps to the south entrance of the Thames Tunnel. Marc Isambard Brunel (1769-1849) finished this tunnel beneath the Thames River in London in 1843.

27

This second problem was most severe in one place where a tunnel would be quite useful—beneath a river. A tunnel under a waterway could provide mass transportation and relieve busy bridge traffic. But the ground beneath rivers was wet and unstable.

In 1802, a group of Englishmen made a heroic attempt to build a very small tunnel beneath the Thames River. But after battling almost constant floods and cave-ins for five years, they had to abandon the project. This led a panel of experts to create a contest to see if anyone could devise a reasonable plan for building a subaqueous, or below water, tunnel. Forty-nine people submitted proposals in 1809. All were rejected. "We consider that an underground tunnel is impracticable," the experts concluded.

The verdict dismayed Marc Isambard Brunel. Although he had no idea how to accomplish the task, he was convinced that it was possible. Several years later, a chance encounter with a piece of rotting shipwood gave him all the inspiration he needed to solve the "impossible" problem.

Marc Brunel was born in Hacqueville, France, in 1769. As a boy, he gained a reputation as a mechanical genius. After observing a ship's quadrant in the cabin of a naval officer, young Marc was able to construct a working version of the complicated navigational instrument. His talent for sketching was so advanced that he astounded friends by drawing perfect circles freehand.

Despite the boy's obvious knack for engineering, his father insisted that he study to become a

subaqueous: made or adapted for underwater use. In Latin, *sub* means under and *aqua* means water.

When it is remembered that [the ship's quadrant Brunel built] demands in the constructor a knowledge not only of geometry, trigonometry, and mechanics, but of optics, one is filled with astonishment and admiration at such intuitive sagacity.
—Richard Beamish,
    Marc Brunel's engineering
    assistant and biographer

priest. Marc entered the seminary of St. Nicaise in Rouen, France, where he did so poorly in his studies that he was sent home. At the age of 16, he sailed for the West Indies to satisfy his curiosity and his craving for adventure. Seven years later, in 1792, he returned to find France in political upheaval. A revolutionary republican government had taken power from the king.

The new leaders strengthened their grip on the country by arresting and executing supporters of the royal family. Brunel's fiancée, Sophie Kingdom, who was English, was imprisoned in a convent. Since Brunel also favored the king, he fled from Paris. For six months, he hid in the town of Rouen, where his cousin was a government official. But revolutionary forces eventually located him and ordered his arrest. Forewarned, Brunel rode furiously toward the port of Le Havre to board a ship sailing for America. Along the way, he fell from his horse and lost the forged passport provided by his cousin that identified him as an agent of the government traveling on official business.

As his ship sailed out of port, a French naval patrol approached. Brunel reached for the passport that would save his life—only to find it missing. With his incredible memory and drawing skill, he reproduced the exact document with all its fancy flourishes by the time the patrol boarded his ship.

Marc Brunel sailed to New York, where he found work surveying the wilderness near Lake Ontario. Again, his cousin helped him. This time he provided Brunel with an introduction to one of

While attempting to flee from France in 1791, King Louis XVI was arrested by republicans at Varennes and forced to return to Paris, where he was later tried for treason and executed.

Alexander Hamilton (1755-1804) was secretary of the treasury under president George Washington. Earlier, Hamilton had founded the Bank of New York and married into a prominent New York family, which made him an influential man.

the most powerful men in the United States, Alexander Hamilton. Hamilton was New York's chief banker at this time. Through Hamilton's connections, Marc Brunel was hired to design many buildings in New York City. He also submitted the winning design for the new Capitol building in Washington, D.C., although the government eventually switched to a less expensive proposal. Within five years of arriving in the United States, Brunel had risen to the position of chief engineer of the state of New York.

In 1798, Brunel learned that his fiancée had escaped from France. He sailed for England in January 1799 to marry her, bringing with him an idea that would greatly simplify the process of manufacturing shipyard pulleys. The British navy spent several years considering his ambitious proposal. Meanwhile, Brunel filled his days by inventing a series of new devices, including a machine that duplicated writing and drawings and a card-shuffling device. After the British approved his plan, Brunel built and set up the pulley-manufacturing machinery. His factory was the first to use the principle of mass production. With only 10 workers, Brunel and his machines could churn out 160,000 pulleys a year, more pulleys than 100 workers could have produced previously.

Even after his factory's success, Brunel's restless mind continued to design useful and profitable machines. He started a sawmill with an invention that could bend and saw timber efficiently. He built a factory that could turn out 400 pairs of shoes a day in nine different sizes with just 24 employees. Brunel was now rich and famous. Many important people, including author Sir Walter Scott and Nicholas, the future tsar of Russia, toured his factories.

Bad luck and poor business sense, however, quickly consumed Brunel's fortune. First, fire destroyed his sawmill. Then he failed to anticipate the end of the War of 1812. Making shoes for the British army as fast as he could, Brunel was left with 80,000 shoes and no buyers when word of the peace treaty reached him. In the end, he had to sell his inventory for almost nothing.

Brunel's misfortunes landed him in debtor's prison on May 14, 1821. Fortunately, British government censors intercepted a letter Brunel had written to Nicholas of Russia. Aware of Brunel's plight and having witnessed his engineering skill, Nicholas wanted him to design a bridge in Russia. Instead, Brunel offered a stunning proposal for a tunnel under the river.

When the British duke of Wellington heard of Brunel's correspondence, he used his influence to get Brunel out of prison. The duke had long been concerned about the mushrooming population on both sides of the Thames River in London, which was causing overcrowding on the ferries and on London Bridge. A tunnel such as the one Brunel had proposed to Nicholas seemed the perfect solution. At last, here was a well-known engineer who said he could build such a tunnel.

In two short hours those most valuable machines, which in point of execution and perfection, exceed everything we know . . . presented the awful sight of a heap of fragments.
—London *Times,* reporting on the fire at Brunel's sawmill

Although a brilliant engineer, Marc Brunel had few business skills. After reviewing Brunel's books, his accountant wrote to him, "It was a most extraordinary jumble, which you certainly have not understood; and I should have wondered if you had. I should hardly have been more surprised if one of your saws had walked to town."

THE BREAKTHROUGH

Brunel had actually found the solution to tunneling underwater in 1816. While installing a sawmill at an English dockyard one autumn afternoon, he spotted a worm-eaten piece of wood from an old ship. He picked it up and found a shipworm burrowing away. Atop the shipworm's head was a shell, shaped something like a shield with jagged edges. As the worm bored, or dug, through the solid oak, its soft body secreted a layer of hard lime in the new passage.

Brunel watched in amazement. This, he realized, was the solution to soft-ground tunneling played out right before his eyes. He spent the next two years designing a device that would mimic the shipworm. In 1818, he patented his "shield"—a huge reinforced iron frame moved by hydraulic presses. As it dug out the space, the shield would provide support for the tunnel's walls. Construction of permanent tunnel walls would then take place under the shield's protection.

After the British Parliament approved the Thames River tunnel project on June 24, 1824, Brunel began constructing his enormous tunnel shield. Then, on February 16, 1825, workers began clearing an acre of land 141 feet (43 meters) from the river bank. Under Brunel's direction, they set out to put in the first shaft. To do this, they built a tower 42 feet (12.8 meters) high and 50 feet (15.2 meters) across. Workers then dug out ground and piled it in the center of the tower, where buckets carried the dirt up and out of the hole. The tower frequently

Iron is the most common metal on Earth. Iron ores are refined in a blast furnace to produce blocks called pig iron, which can then be further refined, remelted, and shaped.

hydraulic: having to do with water or liquids. The word also describes a machine that runs on the pressure of water or liquids.

slipped and had to be adjusted. Not until mid-October, eight months later, did the shaft reach the 63-foot (19.2-meter) depth required for the tunnel. At that point, Brunel brought in the shield. Installation of the huge contraption took about a month. On November 28, the real tunneling began.

Brunel's shield consisted of iron frames joined together and divided to create 36 cells, each space large enough for one worker to wield a shovel. The excavated dirt was put onto long platforms trailing the shield and then removed from the tunnel. Sturdy boards at the top of each cell protected the workers from roof cave-ins. Powerful screw jacks slid the shield forward as the men created space with their digging. At the same time, masons working under the back end of the protective shield sealed up

This cross-section view illustrates Brunel's tunnel shield (C) in action. Under the shield's protection, 36 workers could dig. The dirt was shoveled onto a long platform (A) and then removed. Other workers on the shield bricked up the new opening (B).

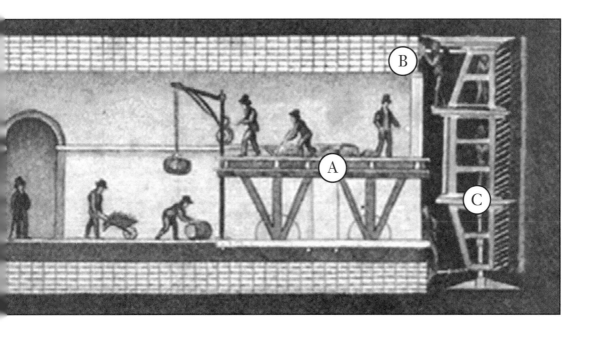

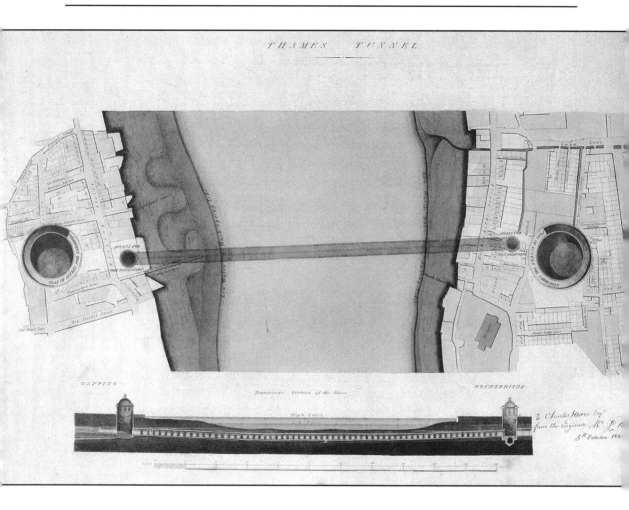

THAMES TUNNEL

WAPPING   *Transverse Section of the River*   *ROTHERHITHE*

Marc Brunel's own drawings of the Thames Tunnel. The small circles at either end of the tunnel were access shafts for pedestrians; carriages used the entrances represented by the larger circles.

the sides and roof of the tunnel with bricks. One observer marveled that the shield operated "like a living thing"—not surprising since Brunel had patterned it after a living shipworm.

Brunel's plan called for digging out a huge tunnel 22 feet (6.7 meters) tall and 38 feet (11.6 meters) wide. This hole would be subdivided into two horseshoe-shaped arches lined with brick. Marc Brunel estimated that digging out the 1,200-foot-long (366-meter) tunnel to these dimensions would take about three years. The Thames Tunnel Company financed the project by selling shares.

According to reports from the ground surveyors, Brunel would have to construct the tunnel fairly close to the river bottom to avoid a large layer of quicksand some 55 feet (16.8 meters) below the river bottom. Their survey turned out to be wrong. Brunel's crews had scarcely begun when a section of the forward wall of the tunnel dissolved into water, quicksand, and gravel. Instead of avoiding the quicksand, they were digging right into it. On January 16, 1826, water gushed into the tunnel. When pumps that removed the water broke down, the water rose to a height of 12 feet (3.7 meters) inside the shield. Twelve days later, another break nearly drowned a worker.

quicksand: loose sand and water forming a soft mass that tends to engulf any object on its surface

With only 14 feet (4.3 meters) of the tunnel dug at this point, Marc Brunel realized he was facing nearly impossible circumstances. But after all the preparation and financial investment, it was too late to turn back. If he was ever going to prove to a skeptical public that he could build his tunnel under the Thames, he had to do it here and now.

Although the quicksand slowed construction, Brunel's shield system kept the project moving forward throughout the spring and into the summer. By mid-August, the tunnel had reached 190 feet (58 meters). At this rate, Marc Brunel would need six years instead of three to finish the job. This was unacceptable to the directors of the Thames Tunnel

Company. They tried to speed up the progress by paying workers according to how fast they advanced. An angry Brunel argued that this would cause shoddy work that could endanger both the workers and the project. But the directors ignored him.

Marc Brunel's fears proved to be well founded. Eager to earn more money, miners cut corners and ignored safety measures. As a result of their carelessness, a section of the ceiling fell out on September 8. More water burst through the walls and even bubbled up from the floor of the tunnel. Brunel and his son, Isambard, the resident engineer on the project, spent over 20 hours a day battling the leaks. Isambard finally collapsed from exhaustion and had to be carried out. At last, after 10 days of frantic effort, the miners had the tunnel patched up.

In May 1827, Brunel received harrowing news. An inspection team probing the river bottom from a diving bell had discovered that the tunnel had veered upwards. Its ceiling was now only inches under the river bottom. If they dug up into the river, the whole project would be ruined.

The men worked gingerly to avoid trouble from above only to have it come at them from a different direction. On May 18, with the tunnel half completed, the forward wall of the tunnel opened up with a roar. A great wave of water, sand, and gravel burst into the tunnel. Miraculously, all of the miners scrambled to safety. But it took nearly the entire summer to pump out the water.

Despite the frustrations caused by the many leaks, Brunel pronounced his invention a success.

The water came in a great wave. . . . The whole work, which only a few short hours before had commanded the homage of an admiring public, was consigned to darkness and solitude. The men filled the staircase. With the utmost difficulty the lowest flight of steps was cleared, when . . . the recoil came and surged just under our feet. The men now hurried up the stairs. The roll was now called, when to our unspeakable joy, every man answered to his name.
—Richard Beamish,
   describing the
   May 18 flood

He wrote in his diary, "My confidence in the shield is not only undiminished; it is, on the contrary, tried with its full effect." In other words, under the worst possible conditions, the shield continued to slowly advance the tunnel. As Brunel noted, without the shield protecting the workers, the tunnel would never have had a chance of being completed.

Men descended to the river floor from inside a diving bell (attached to the chain). Using long sticks, they measured the depth of the river bottom above the top of the tunnel.

Upon hearing the tunnel was full of water a second time, Richard Beamish had opened a staircase and descended two steps when the rushing water pushed Isambard Brunel right into his arms. Severely injured, Brunel was unable to work for several months.

Having passed the halfway point, Marc Brunel believed that they had gone through the worst that could be expected. But on January 12, 1828, his greatest fear came to pass. The ground popped like someone had pulled a plug, and the Thames River began pouring through a gap into the tunnel. Six men died in the disaster.

Brunel directed 4,500 bags of clay and gravel to be dumped from boats to plug the hole in the river-bed, but it was too late. After this latest disaster, the financiers had no more stomach for the project. In two and a half years of digging, construction had barely passed the halfway point. The directors ordered the tunnel sealed. Rather than removing the massive shield, they simply walled it in with bricks.

Marc Brunel, however, was not ready to give up on the project. He pointed out that the tunnel still stood where the brick had been laid under his shield system and pleaded for backers to help him finish. But people only remembered the unfinished portion and the terrible flooding that had constantly plagued the project. Brunel's unfinished tunnel now became the object of jokes.

After almost a decade of inaction, the duke of Wellington once again came to Brunel's rescue by arranging a government loan. In 1837, workers opened the tunnel and removed the old shield. Brunel installed a new, stronger shield in its place, and the tunnel again inched forward into the soggy earth.

By this time, Brunel was in his late sixties and in poor health. Isambard Brunel was pursuing his own engineering career and no longer helping his father. During the previous construction, Marc Brunel had gone into the tunnel every few hours during each night to inspect the progress. But now Sophie Brunel refused to allow her husband to follow such an exhausting schedule. Brunel compromised. He lived only a few yards from the entrance to the tunnel. Every two hours, when a bell by his bedside rang, Brunel hauled up a basket on a string that contained a report of the latest progress.

Problems continued to plague Marc Brunel and his workers. In addition to frequent leaks, poisonous gas seeped into the tunnel. Brunel installed fans for ventilation and shortened the miners' work shifts.

By October, the tunnelers had advanced far enough to begin digging the shaft on the opposite shore to connect with the tunnel. Again, they ran into bad luck. The ground was full of iron tools and scraps from the days when a shipyard stood on the spot. Digging out all this iron took so long that, after a year of hard work, the shaft was only 7 feet (2.1 meters) deep.

Finally, in December 1842, the shaft linked up with the tunnel. On March 25, 1843, more than 18 years after the project was started, officials opened the Thames Tunnel.

A gifted engineer like his father, Isambard Kingdom Brunel (1806-1859) was best known for the design and construction of steamships. He also worked for the railroads, laying 1,000 miles (1,610 kilometers) of track throughout Great Britain and Ireland.

An arched corridor of apparently interminable length, gloomily lighted with jets of gas at regular intervals—plastered at the sides and stone beneath the feet. . . . It would have made an admirable prison.
—American author Nathaniel Hawthorne, describing the Thames Tunnel

The Thames Tunnel was well ahead of its time. Yet when congratulated on his achievement, Marc Brunel simply stated, "If I had to do it over again, I'd do better."

THE RESULT

The long-awaited Thames Tunnel attracted so much attention that 50,000 people passed through it during the first 24 hours it was open. In its first four months of existence, more than 1 million people paid the penny toll to make the journey under the river through the brick-lined tunnel.

Ironically, once the difficult part of the project—the tunneling—was finished, the easier task of installing highway approaches into the tunnel was delayed. Brunel died in 1849 without ever seeing the tunnel put to the heavy traffic use he had envisioned. For 23 years, the Thames Tunnel was used exclusively by pedestrians. During the day, the tunnel was like an underground street market filled with stalls and artists. But at night, it became the refuge

of the homeless, who called the tunnel the Hades Hotel for the Greek name for the underworld.

In 1865, the East London Railway Company bought the tunnel, installed rails, and made it a part of the London subway system. Brunel had constructed his tunnel so solidly that trains continue to run through the tunnel today.

The most important contribution Marc Brunel made in building the Thames Tunnel was the demonstration of his revolutionary shield. Other engineers have altered and improved on his design, but the basic concept of the system Brunel borrowed from the shipworm continues to serve as the foundation of soft-ground tunneling projects, including the massive "Chunnel" beneath the English Channel. Connecting England and France, this train tunnel opened in 1992.

Marc Brunel's work also inspired the use of subways for transportation in congested cities and provided the technology to construct them.

CHAPTER THREE

John and Washington Roebling and the Brooklyn Bridge

The bustling business district of New York City's Manhattan Island stood only 1,600 feet (488 meters) away. Yet, for the ferry commuters from Brooklyn, it might as well have been halfway around the world. During the winter of 1866-1867, bitter north winds had frozen much of the East River. Boats that normally ferried one-tenth of Brooklyn's population across the water each day were stuck in the ice that choked the docks.

John Roebling proposed a solution to those who desperately needed transportation to Manhattan Island and back. It was the same suggestion he had been making for more than a decade: Why not construct a bridge over the East River? Others had proposed the same solution as early as 1800, but people had looked over the wide expanse of the East River and quickly dismissed the suggestion. Now, frustrated by the exceptionally bad weather, New Yorkers finally decided to consider Roebling's proposal.

John Roebling (1806-1869), at left, and his son Washington Roebling (1837-1926) linked New York City and Brooklyn with a bridge that few believed could be built.

A bridge constructed at Wheeling, West Virginia, in 1849 served as a grim reminder that engineers sometimes promised more than they could deliver. Only five years after this magnificent 1,000-foot (305-meter) suspension bridge over the Ohio River had been completed, a fierce storm tore it to shreds.

A **suspension bridge** features a roadway suspended from cables that are held up by towers and anchored at each end.

Many legislators took a deep breath before casting their vote on the Brooklyn bridge project. After all, Roebling proposed to build a suspension bridge nearly 600 feet (183 meters) longer than the longest bridge in the world at that time. Many engineering experts said the bridge could not be built, or if it were built, would not hold up. The legislators decided, however, to put their trust in Roebling and approved the project.

John Augustus Roebling had come a long way in his engineering career. He was born on June 12, 1806, to middle-class German parents and grew up in the town of Mühlhausen in an area of Germany then known as Prussia. John's parents were able to provide him with an outstanding education at the Polytechnic Institute in Berlin. While enrolled at the institute, the 17-year-old Roebling saw a small example of a new type of bridge called a suspension bridge. Fascinated by the design of the bridge, Roebling studied engineering.

Upon finishing his education in 1826, John Roebling took a job as an assistant engineer. He quickly grew tired of government regulations and his superiors' refusal to allow him to use innovations in engineering. In May 1831, along with his brother Karl and a group of 53 friends who shared his frustration with the government, Roebling boarded a ship for the United States. The group bought 7,000 acres in western Pennsylvania where they established their own community of Saxonburg.

For a time, Roebling joined his neighbors in farming. He married Johanna Herting in 1836 and the next year the first of their seven children, Washington Augustus, was born. But eventually John Roebling tired of farming and longed to get back into engineering. His opportunity came in 1837 when he found work on the Sandy and Beaver branch of the Pennsylvania Canal.

Since boats provided the easiest and cheapest means of shipping goods, Americans at that time were building many canals to connect waterways. In low-lying areas, this involved little more than cutting ditches into the land. Where mountains blocked the way, workers assembled small sections of track. Boats could then be loaded onto railway cars and be mechanically hauled up and over the mountains on these tracks. This operation required hemp ropes up to nine inches thick. But even ropes as sturdy as these eventually wore out.

hemp: a plant, the fibers of which are used to make strong rope or coarse cloth

In 1841, Roebling was watching a crew pull a boat over one of these hills when the rope broke,

A canal boat being hauled over the Allegheny Mountains, part of the Pennsylvania Portage Railway

sending the boat hurtling down the hill to destruction. Roebling had a sudden inspiration. He had recently read an article in a German magazine about a new invention—rope made of strands of iron wire. A superstrong rope made of wire, Roebling noted, could support far greater weight than the standard hemp rope. Wire rope, or cable, would be a great advantage in construction.

Since reports of the wire rope had been published only in Europe, Roebling was the first American to pursue this technology. He invented his own wire-rope-making machine and trained some of his neighbors in Saxonburg to run it.

At first, people were skeptical of the odd-looking rope. Eventually, though, Roebling was able to persuade canal engineers to try his product. Worried that their control over the rope market was slipping away, Kentucky hemp producers fought back hard and dirty, secretly cutting some of his wires. But the superior strength of iron for heavy construction work was so obvious that Roebling's wire cable soon replaced hemp ropes on many construction projects. His innovation helped establish him as a leading canal engineer in the eastern United States.

In 1844, John Roebling finally got a chance to try his hand at his first engineering love—building a suspension bridge. He used iron cables to construct a bridge over the Allegheny River in Pittsburgh, and then a second bridge over the nearby Monongahela River. While working on these bridges, he began to perfect a new method of installing the cables. Instead of putting the wires together on the ground

Workers wrapping strands of wire together to form a cable

to form a cable and then lifting the cable into position, Roebling assembled the cables in place. He strung one strand of iron wire from one end of the bridge to the other, then went back over it with another wire. After many trips back and forth, he had enough strands to twist into a sturdy cable.

Roebling was so busy with his projects that in one letter to Charles Swan, his plant manager, he wrote something that revealed he was unaware of the birth of one of his children. By 1850, Roebling had finished six wire-cable suspension bridges and had relocated to Trenton, New Jersey, where he owned a thriving wire-rope factory.

The following year, John Roebling began work on his most challenging project to date—a two-level bridge over the spectacular gorge below Niagara Falls in New York. Railroad cars would use the upper level, while horse and carriage traffic could travel on the lower section. Prior to this, no suspension bridge had ever been built for railway traffic. Anxiety increased in May 1854 when the famous Wheeling, West Virginia, suspension bridge collapsed under high winds.

But Roebling claimed there were faults in the Wheeling Bridge's design that caused its destruction. The builders had not allowed for vibrations caused by strong winds. Roebling insisted his bridge would stand. On March 16, 1855, a train chugged across his newly completed Niagara Bridge. Like all of Roebling's bridges, this one held firm.

This success established Roebling as one of the leading bridge builders in the country. Community leaders in Pittsburgh and Cincinnati sought him out for major bridges. In both of these projects, he had the help of his son Washington. In 1857, the younger Roebling had been one of the first graduates of Rensselaer Polytechnic Institute, a pioneering engineering school in Troy, New York.

The Cincinnati Bridge was an especially ambitious project. The plans called for a 1,057-foot (322-meter) suspension bridge over the Ohio River—longer than any bridge ever built to date. Work began in 1856, but it was interrupted by the economic panic of 1857 and again by the U.S. Civil War (1861-1865).

You drive over the Suspension Bridge and divide your misery between the chances of smashing down 200 feet into the river below, and the chances of having a railway-train overhead smashing down onto you.
—Mark Twain, American author, commenting on the Niagara Bridge

Washington Roebling enlisted in the Union army in 1861 and worked as an engineering officer under General G. K. Warren. In 1864, Washington met and immediately fell in love with Warren's sister, Emily, at an officers' ball. Discharged from the army in December 1864, Washington Roebling married Emily Warren the following month.

As the war wound down in the spring of 1865, the Roeblings returned to Cincinnati to resume construction on the bridge. Father and son finally completed their work late in 1866, and the bridge opened on New Year's Day 1867. Worn out by the 11-year project, the 61-year old John Roebling announced that he was ready to "leave bridge-building to younger folks."

But scarcely had he finished at Cincinnati when an even more challenging project came his way. The New York state legislature had decided to fund Roebling's long-standing desire to build a bridge over the East River from Brooklyn to Manhattan.

Government officials appointed John Roebling as chief engineer for the Brooklyn Bridge in the spring of 1867. Roebling promised he could build this bridge safely for any kind of traffic—trains, horses, carriages, and pedestrians—at a reasonable cost without obstructing boat traffic during the construction. He enthusiastically declared that his project "will not only be the greatest bridge in existence, but it will be the greatest engineering work of this continent, and of the age."

"It was the first time I ever saw her," Washington Roebling (above) wrote to his sister Elvira after meeting Emily Warren (below) at a ball, *"and I am very much of the opinion that she has captured your brother Washy's heart."*

THE BREAKTHROUGH

But neither Roebling's confidence nor the fact that the government had authorized the project persuaded the public that such a grand bridge could be built. Roebling spent two years arguing in favor of and then revising his plans before the skeptical Board of Consulting Engineers would approve his design.

One of the stumbling blocks was Roebling's decision to use steel cables instead of iron cables. Steel—an alloy of iron with small amounts of the common, nonmetallic chemical element carbon, plus traces of other elements—was then a relatively untested material. Yet, Roebling insisted, this material would work better than iron as a structural support.

At last, John Roebling was able to begin preliminary work in the early summer of 1869. The first thing he needed was to determine the location of the two main towers from which the cables would be strung. One June morning, he stood on pilings near a ferry dock on the Brooklyn shore, attempting to calculate the exact site of the Brooklyn tower.

alloy: a mixture of one metal with another, such as brass, which is an alloy of copper and zinc, or a mix of one metal with a nonmetal. Alloys are useful because their characteristics are often quite different from the pure metals from which they are made.

The steel cables Roebling proposed were almost 16 inches (40.6 centimeters) in diameter. Strands were formed by tying together almost 300 steel wires, each the thickness of pencil lead. Each cable consisted of 19 of these strands (A) wrapped (B) and pressed together (C).

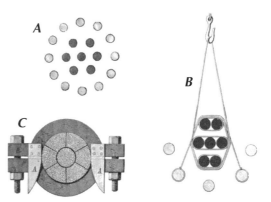

While he was taking signals from an assistant on the New York side, a ferry approached the shore. It was going too fast and, unable to stop in time, the ferry smashed the protective fender on the shore, causing the timbers to shift. Roebling's foot was caught in the wood and crushed so badly that his toes had to be amputated. Tetanus then set in, and Roebling died on July 22. The genius behind the Brooklyn Bridge was gone before construction even began. After this tragedy, the burden of the project suddenly fell on John's son Washington.

The most difficult part of the job would be digging down to bedrock on the banks of the river to provide a solid base for the towers. Washington's first major decision was to use pneumatic caissons (KAYsons) to accomplish this task.

A caisson is a huge watertight cylinder with a floorless chamber. Pneumatic means that air is pumped into the cylinder to allow the workers to breathe. The two caissons used for the Brooklyn Bridge were huge—three stories tall and large enough to cover a city block. Made of wood and iron by a shipyard on the East River, then sealed to be waterproof, the caissons were launched down a ramp into the river just like a ship. Towed by tugboats to the tower sites, the caissons were then sunk. The bottom edges of Washington Roebling's caissons were honed to a sharp edge so that they could cut deep into the ground as pressure was applied from above. As the workers dug, the caissons would sink deeper and deeper until they hit solid footing. They would then be filled with concrete and become

Bedrock is the solid rock of the Earth's crust that usually lies under layers of topsoil, sand, and small rocks.

The **caisson** originated in France, as did the name, meaning "chest" or "large box." An airlock that enabled workers to climb in and out of a sealed chamber filled with compressed air had been devised as early as 1831 by the British admiral Lord Thomas Cochrane. In 1851, the first pneumatic caissons were used to lay a bridge foundation under the Medway River in Rochester, England.

Workers stand on the Brooklyn caisson before it was sent to the bottom of the East River to provide the foundation for the tower.

Concrete is a building material made from **cement** (a powder of crushed limestone and clay), sand, pebbles, and water. It hardens into a rocklike substance.

the underwater foundations for the two bridge towers. Limestone blocks were then piled on top up to the waterline.

To work properly, a pneumatic caisson must be absolutely airtight. Workers can enter it only through two airlock shafts in the roof. Any leaks can cause pressurized air to escape, after which water rushes in. This happened once in the Brooklyn caisson. Compressed air suddenly shot out of the caisson, spewing water, mud, and rocks 500 feet (152 meters) in the air. The noise and the mud that rained over Brooklyn for blocks caused a panic. Fortunately, the accident occurred on a Sunday when no one was in the caisson. Afterwards, workers sealed the caisson, pumped out the water, and went back to work.

The ground beneath the caisson on the Brooklyn side proved incredibly hard. Despite having 360 men working around the clock six days a week, rotating in eight-hour shifts, Roebling's crew managed to dig out only 6 inches (15 centimeters) in a week. Realizing he could never get the bridge built at that rate, Roebling took a major chance. He decided to risk blasting the rock with gunpowder inside the caisson. No one had ever used explosives under high air pressure before. Rather than making his workers be the guinea pigs, Roebling undertook the experiments himself to see if it could be done safely. First, he fired his revolver in the caisson. Then he lit small batches of gunpowder. Eventually, he worked his way up to the large charges he needed to blast out rock. He found that under careful conditions, he could blast safely.

While Washington Roebling prevented major fires from occurring in the caissons, a minor fire nearly ruined the project. In December 1870, some exposed caulking in the ceiling caught fire. It burned for hours before workers detected it. Roebling spent an entire night in the caisson, locating and fighting hidden fires.

After Roebling had gone home, his workers drilled through some of the wood in the caisson roof and found more live coals. Roebling returned and ordered the caisson to be flooded. It remained full of water for days. When they pumped the water out

The Brooklyn caisson was hot, humid, noisy, and lit only with limelights that burned calcium oxide, a mineral powder called lime. The underwater pressure made the workers' voices sound faint and high.

Caulking is a material used to seal or fill seams and cracks to make something airtight or watertight. For example, the seams of a wooden ship are filled with tar or pitch.

In each caisson, there were two airlocks (the center shafts) for the workers to enter and exit, two supply shafts, and two water shafts (the larger openings that extend up on either end) into which men shoveled debris.

and refilled the caisson with air, the workers found that the charred sections had greatly weakened the structure. They had to cut out these sections and caulk, or fill them in. The repairs were completed on March 6, 1871. Five days later, the caisson was filled with concrete.

Launched on May 8, 1871, the New York caisson posed even more difficult conditions than the Brooklyn one had. Although the excavation was easier, the workers dug into what turned out to be a former dump. The stench was so overpowering that

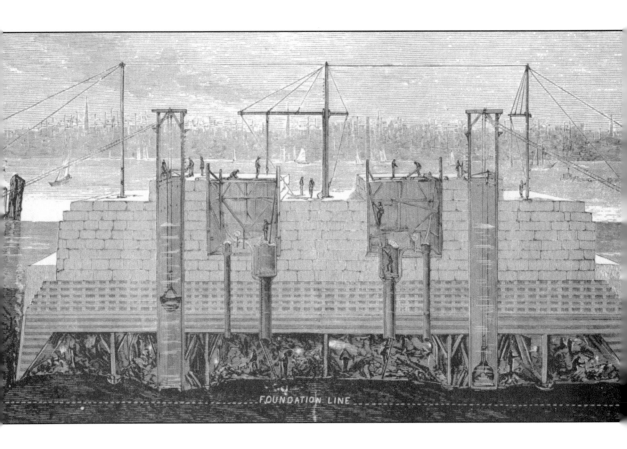

FOUNDATION LINE

some men lost consciousness and had to be carried out. The workers also encountered quicksand that made progress difficult.

But the worst danger by far was something known as the bends. This life-threatening condition causes pain and paralysis and occurs when people move too quickly between environments of widely varying air pressure. While the Brooklyn caisson struck bedrock and digging could stop at 44 feet (13.4 meters), the New York caisson went past 70 feet (21.3 meters) without striking bedrock. The greater depth required greater air pressure inside the caisson and this led to the bends.

In the first five months of 1872, three workers died from the bends. More than 100 suffered from its effects before the caisson rested on solid ground at 78 feet (23.8 meters). Among those stricken was Washington Roebling, who was carried out of the New York caisson in the summer of 1872. He lay near death for two days from his attack of the bends. Afterwards, he was racked with terrible pains that recurred for years.

At first, Roebling kept his condition secret and was able to work three or four days a week. But by December 1872, he was very ill. He spent the winter painstakingly writing out instructions for finishing the bridge because he feared he would not live long enough to see it finished. The Roeblings traveled to Europe, hoping spas that offered water treatments would cure Washington. Still ill, he returned to Trenton. For three more years, Roebling continued to supervise the bridge construction through

People afflicted with **the bends** often walked stooped over from excruciating stomach cramps. This symptom gave the condition its name. When underwater, the pressure begins to dissolve nitrogen gas in a person's blood. If this pressure is suddenly relieved, the nitrogen again becomes gas and can form bubbles that block oxygen in the blood stream. The lack of oxygen to vital body parts causes the intense pain of the bends. If the pressure is relieved gradually—decompression—the gas forms slowly and is released by the lungs.

Today scientists know the safe rate of decompression is more than a minute for every pound of pressure. At 65 feet (19.8 meters) down, the New York caisson workers should have spent 20 minutes decompressing in the lock instead of the average 2 or 3.

correspondence, all the while suffering from terrible headaches and pains in his stomach, joints, arms, and legs. Because of his absence, there was much public skepticism about his ability to finish the job.

But Roebling was determined to see his father's project completed. In 1876, the Roeblings returned to New York so Washington could more closely supervise the cable work. He rented a house from which he could watch the work progress through binoculars. Emily turned out to have a brilliant mind for mathematics and engineering. While caring for her husband's health, she had also been assisting him with his correspondence and other work. She now became a valuable link between the supervisors and the project, relaying Washington's instructions, inspecting the progress, and reporting back to her husband.

Each of the gigantic towers took five years to construct. Looming 276 feet (84 meters) above the river, they were equal in height to a 25-story building at a time when structures were rarely over 5 stories tall. The Brooklyn tower was finished in 1875 and the New York tower the following year. Next came the job of stringing cables. Roebling stuck with his father's radical proposal of using steel cables, coated with zinc to protect them from rust.

The job went more smoothly than the tower construction. To avoid entangling the river traffic, Roebling cleverly laid steel strands—composed of 300 wires wrapped together to form a cable 16 inches (40.6 centimeters) in diameter—on the bottom of the river. At the right moment, when all was clear,

Master mechanic E. F. Farrington doffed his hat to the crowd that gathered to watch him become the first person to ride the traveler rope between the Brooklyn and New York towers in August 1876.

The Brooklyn tower climbs brick by brick toward its final height of 276 feet (84 meters).

he raised a strand to be strung between the two towers and anchored to the ground behind the towers.

The immense anchorages on either end of the bridge were crucial because they held the main cables from which the bridge would be suspended. Beneath each structure, which was as large as a city block and nine stories tall, were buried four massive cast-iron anchor plates, one for each cable. This anchorage system, still used in suspension bridges today, was first employed by John Roebling.

Yet there were problems with this part of the work as well. Roebling discovered that one of his cable suppliers was cheating him by substituting poor quality wire for the specified wire. By the time Roebling caught the error, he could not afford to dismantle the bridge and start over with new wire.

Workers attach floor beams to the suspenders hanging from the cables.

All he could do was add enough extra wire to make up for the weakness of the deficient wire. Accidents also continued to plague the projects. Tools were dropped on other workers, and high winds blew men to their deaths. Several men were killed when one cable suddenly snapped.

As the project dragged on in the 1880s, the skeptics began to get the upper hand. Roebling had already spent more than twice what his father originally estimated for the Brooklyn Bridge. At one point, construction stopped for six months while officials debated the wisdom of pouring more money into this seemingly endless project. When, in 1881, Roebling decided to add 1,000 tons (910 metric tons) of steel into the trusses holding the flooring of the bridge, he was sharply criticized. The *New York Times* labeled Roebling's decision "stupidity," believing that such extra weight would cause the bridge to collapse. Government officials tried to fire Roebling.

But Roebling weathered the storm of controversy, and his tireless public relations efforts kept the funding from drying up. On May 24, 1883, the sun shone and schools and stores closed for the day. Still quite ill, Roebling sat at his windows, watching through his binoculars as President Chester A. Arthur dedicated the completed Brooklyn Bridge. The president then walked across the bridge from the Manhattan side to Brooklyn, where Emily Roebling greeted him. That evening, fireworks launched from both towers lit the skies for over an hour. Roebling himself had never set foot on the bridge.

When approved for construction, the bridge had no official name. John Roebling referred to it as the East River Bridge in his proposal. Earlier, some had called it the Empire Bridge. The organization incorporated to build it was the New York Bridge Company. But others also called it the Roebling Bridge or the Great Bridge or the Brooklyn Bridge, the name that finally stuck.

THE RESULT

The Brooklyn Bridge proved its value immediately. In its first day of existence, more than 150,000 people crossed over the East River. Just five years after it was built, trains carried 30 million passengers a year across the bridge. The trip across took five minutes and cost five cents. The easy access to Manhattan helped Brooklyn grow until, by the turn of the century, it was the third largest city in the country. Eventually, Brooklyn became incorporated into New York City.

As for its engineering significance, John and Washington Roebling constructed the first bridge made from steel, a material that proved to be far superior to iron. John Roebling also proved a point that he had often made in response to criticism of his Brooklyn Bridge proposal. "A span of 1,600 feet or more can be made just as safe, and as strong in proportion, as a span of 100 feet," he had insisted. The Roeblings constructed their bridge so solidly that in spite of the unanticipated addition of automobile traffic, it held up without the need for reinforcement for more than 70 years.

Washington Roebling slowly recovered from the illness that had plagued him for so long and lived to age 89. The bridge project done, he ran his father's steel wire business for many years. He and Emily named their son John Augustus Roebling after his grandfather. Emily Roebling, a pioneer in her own right, later earned a law degree when she was 55 years old. She died in 1903.

The Brooklyn Bridge was the forerunner of the modern long-span bridges that today grace the world's rivers, bays, and straits. It was so far ahead of its time that nearly 50 years passed before anyone attempted a significantly longer bridge. *Scientific American* magazine summed up the Roeblings' achievement by calling their bridge "the grandest piece of engineering the world has ever seen." It was also a beautiful bridge with high arches in the stone towers and electric lamps lighting the outline of the structure at night, for among its many merits, it was the first bridge to use electric illumination.

"This part I call the elevated promenade," John Roebling said about the pedestrian boardwalk 18 feet (5.5 meters) above the bridge, "because its principal use will be to allow people of leisure . . . to promenade over the bridge on fine days, in order to enjoy the beautiful views and the pure air."

CHAPTER FOUR

Alexandre Gustave Eiffel and the Eiffel Tower

In the late 1870s, French government officials brainstormed to come up with spectacular ways to celebrate the 100th anniversary of the French Revolution. They decided to hold a "Universal Exposition of the Products of Industry" in 1889, and Edouard Lockroy, the minister of commerce and industry, proposed the construction of a 300-meter tower as a symbol of France's industrial progress. (They chose the nearest round metric equivalent to 1,000 feet.)

This was certainly the kind of grand gesture called for by the occasion. But was it practical? The highest human-made structure ever attempted was the Washington Monument in the United States. Begun in 1848, the construction had run into so many problems that it was still not finished (and wouldn't be until 1884).

Now Lockroy was proposing a structure nearly double the height of the 555-foot (169-meter)

When completed in 1889, the iron tower Alexandre Gustave Eiffel (1832-1923) raised in Paris was the tallest structure in the world. The Eiffel Tower held this distinction for 40 years.

monument. Furthermore, there were aesthetic concerns. Who wanted a huge ugly building cluttering up the skyline of the beautiful city of Paris? Officials hedged and delayed until it was almost too late. When they finally announced the contest, contenders had only 16 days to submit their proposals.

The entries included some designs that were exactly the type of monstrosities the officials wanted to avoid. There was a plan for a giant guillotine—the gruesome symbol of the bloody French Revolution. Another architect envisioned a huge lawn sprinkler that could water all the gardens of Paris. Fortunately, a proposal arrived from a man with both some artistic sense and practical knowledge of how to build a tower nearly twice as high as ever attempted before. Alexandre Eiffel's tower was the star attraction of the centennial celebration and it lives on today as the symbol of one of the world's most famous cities.

Alexandre Gustave Boenickhausen-Eiffel was born on December 15, 1832, in Dijon, France. (He would shorten his last name to Eiffel in 1880.) His father, François Alexandre Boenickhausen-Eiffel, had been a soldier before his marriage to Catherine-Mélanie Moneuse. His mother had by far the most influence on Alexandre's life. The daughter of a timber merchant, Catherine had a good head for business, something that her husband lacked. It was she who organized and ran a successful coal business, which she sold in 1843 at a handsome profit. She also oversaw Alexandre's education and later arranged his marriage and helped him start his own business.

Alexandre had little interest in school, which left him with "the most wretched memories." As a child, he became close to his uncle, Jean-Baptiste Mollerat, a chemist who operated a vinegar and paint factory. Mollerat interested Alexandre in his business and offered to let him manage the company when he retired. With this incentive, Alexandre prepared for a career in chemical engineering at the École Centrale des Arts et Manufactures.

Before he completed his schooling, however, his father and Uncle Mollerat quarreled bitterly. Mollerat withdrew his offer of employment for his nephew. Without the incentive of a secure job, Eiffel now switched to a subject that he found more interesting—metallurgy, the study of metals.

metallurgy: the science and technology of metals, including mining and refining of metals from their ores, making alloys, and shaping metals

After finishing school, Eiffel landed a job in 1856 as a private secretary to Charles Nepveu, a prominent railroad construction engineer. Eiffel's time with Nepveu was brief but crucial to his career. Nepveu allowed him access to his files, so Eiffel could study all aspects of construction engineering. The employer also introduced his young secretary to some of the most powerful people in the business. A year later, Nepveu sold out to a large Belgian firm, General Railway Equipment Company, which hired both Nepveu and Eiffel.

One of Eiffel's first tasks was to design a metal bridge. The company was bidding on a contract to construct such a bridge over the Garonne River in Bordeaux. This was an important project that would link two major railroads. But shortly after Eiffel began work on the project, the company's chief engineer was suddenly fired. When, in 1858, the company won the Bordeaux contract, it had no experienced engineer to lead the project. Alexandre Eiffel proved to be such a good organizer and careful planner that he quickly assumed command of constructing the bridge.

Eiffel's area of expertise was in metal construction, not in bridge building, so he had to learn his craft quickly. For example, he used hydraulic presses to sink piles, a technique he had read about but never tried before. The bridge he designed at Bordeaux consisted of a metal superstructure 1,550 feet (472 meters) long that was held in place by six 78-foot (23.8-meter) piers, or vertical supports. Despite his inexperience, Eiffel brought the project to completion on schedule in 1860. He also earned the respect of his workers by diving into the Garonne River to save a riveter who had fallen from the bridge.

Eiffel's success encouraged him to go into business on his own. In 1864, backed by his mother's money, he organized a small metal construction business in the Paris suburb of Levallois-Perret. There he made metal boilers and, he said in his advertisements, "any metal construction you may need." Two years later, he expanded his business with financing provided by business partners. The company branched into building portable bridges for the army and small bridges for private landowners. During this time, Alexandre Eiffel was constantly researching the qualities of metal—its strength, durability, and flexibility. Before long, he knew as much about metal construction as any man alive.

Eiffel's performance at Bordeaux impressed people throughout the industry, but not the young women he was dating, for French high society looked down upon the young engineer's profession. Eiffel proposed marriage to four different women in one year; all yielded to family pressure and turned him down. He recovered from these humiliations to marry Marie Gaudelet, the granddaughter of one of his parents' business partners, in 1862. Happy together, they had five children before her death in 1877.

Eiffel struggled for over eight years to keep his business afloat. Then, in 1875, he won two huge contracts. One of these was a railroad bridge over the Duoro River in Oporto, Portugal. The river was so deep, ran so rapidly, and flooded so frequently that there was no hope of constructing piers in the river. This had discouraged many engineers from attempting the bridge, but Eiffel proposed building arches toward each other so the two sides of the arch met in the middle. Upon this arch, he would construct a large central span.

Eiffel's second major project was a new railroad station in Pest, Hungary. Eiffel cleverly built the metal frame of the new station over the old station (which was removed at the end of the project) so that service was not interrupted during the two-year construction period.

These two projects earned Alexandre Gustave Eiffel fame as Europe's master metal builder, and his company soon had more business than it could handle. Perhaps his most interesting project involved the Statue of Liberty. Frédéric Bartholdi, who designed the 151-foot (46-meter) statue, was a sculptor, not an engineer. He knew what he wanted to build, but he did not know how to provide the structural support needed for this heavy statue covered with copper plates. Bartholdi turned to the metal expert, Eiffel, who built a light iron and steel skeleton for the statue in 1881.

An **arch** is a structure shaped like an upside-down U. The upper edge can be curved, pointed, or flat, and it usually supports the weight above it, such as the roadway of the **arch bridge** over the Duoro River.

Alexandre Eiffel provided the iron and steel skeleton for the Statue of Liberty. The statue has stood in New York Harbor since 1886, welcoming millions of immigrants to the United States.

THE BREAKTHROUGH

When the French government announced the competition for the centennial tower, two of Eiffel's company engineers, Maurice Koechlin and Emile Nouguier, and architect Stephen Sauvestre came to Eiffel with a preliminary plan. Eiffel liked what he saw and immediately recognized that his company had a tremendous advantage over the competition. Such an enormous tower, he figured, would have to be made of metal. Iron was stronger than wood and stone. Yet it was elastic and light enough to keep the structure from crushing itself with its own weight. After reviewing his engineers' plans, Eiffel took over the project.

The Eiffel design easily won the bid. On January 8, 1887, Eiffel signed a contract to construct the tower for $1.5 million (7.8 million francs). Eiffel also promised to complete the tower in two years—in time for the centennial. Under this tight deadline, work began on the foundation on January 26. Eiffel constructed massive stone foundations, one in each corner of a square. The square covered four acres on a cleared site in a park called Champ de Mars beside the Seine River. Upon these foundations, he began building four giant pillars that slanted inward.

The Eiffel name lent credibility to the fantastic tower proposal. Given Eiffel's flawless record of achievement, few doubted he could build what he proposed. A great many people, however, doubted that Eiffel *should* build what he proposed. Some residents with homes bordering the construction area

tried to get the courts to stop the project. They feared the huge tower would fall, an idea supported by a mathematics professor who calculated the tower would topple before it reached 750 feet (229 meters). Even if the tower stood, neighbors feared their lives and property would be in danger from tools, rivets, and other metal pieces dropped from the great height of the tower.

The engineer assured people that the tower was less likely to collapse on itself than virtually any other building around. Considering its size, it was

One of the pillars that formed a corner of the Eiffel Tower, January 1887

relatively light, and it was designed to distribute the weight so evenly that the pressure on the foundation would be no greater in any given area than the pressure exerted on the floor by a large man sitting on a chair. He further eased fears by declaring he would personally pay for any damages or injuries caused by the construction.

Others opposed the project for different reasons. Work had barely begun before 47 of Paris's most prominent artists, writers, painters, musicians, and architects published a letter denouncing the "erection in the heart of our capital of the useless and monstrous Eiffel Tower." The protesters called it an "odious column of bolted metal."

Eiffel responded tactfully to the criticism of the tower being an eyesore, pointing to the great pyramids of Egypt. No one ridiculed those massive towers, so why was it that "what is admired in Egypt would become hideous and ridiculous in Paris?"

Alexandre Eiffel had some important decisions to make early in the project. First, he had a choice of three kinds of metal for his structure: cast iron, wrought iron, or steel. Concluding that cast iron was too brittle for such a tall tower and steel too flexible, he chose wrought iron.

The next problem involved keeping the foundation absolutely level. An error too small for the human eye to notice would become magnified as the building grew taller. Eiffel was aware that such a problem had delayed completion of the Washington Monument. Although the monument's foundation had been thought to be perfectly level, by the time

Iron ores are refined in a blast furnace to produce blocks called pig iron, which can be remelted and poured into molds to make **cast iron**, or commercially purified to make **wrought iron**, or alloyed with carbon and other elements to make **steel**. Iron corrodes in moist air and becomes rust, or iron oxide. Iron can be galvanized, or coated, with zinc or paint to slow down rusting.

the building reached 143 feet (44 meters), it had an obvious lean. In a tower twice the height of the monument, such an error would be disastrous.

Eiffel eliminated any problem with levelness by installing enormous hydraulic jacks in each of the four corners of the tower. Each jack used water under such tremendous pressure that it could lift 900 tons (819 metric tons). This allowed Eiffel to adjust the corners at any time to correct for errors that might show up later.

The problem that concerned Alexandre Eiffel the most, however, was the wind. He was aware that the tower would be reaching up into a region where strong winds often blow, and the force of such winds could eventually topple even a fairly stable tower. To solve that issue, he built enough open space into his metal supports for the wind to blow through the structure. By Eiffel's calculations, the tower could withstand hurricane force winds of 148 miles (238 kilometers) per hour.

Eiffel went about every phase of the construction with painstaking care because he knew the smallest errors could cause great damage. He had his engineers draw separate plans for each wrought iron piece that would form the tower—5,329 mechanical drawings were required to produce the 18,038 pieces. The distance between rivet holes was precisely measured to within .0039 inches (.1 millimeters). Eiffel then had the metal pieces manufactured and drilled at the workshops in Levallois-Perret. Leaving no room for improvising or "making do," he ordered his crew to return any

rivet: a metal bolt with a head on one end inserted through aligned holes in the pieces to be joined and then hammered on the plain end to form a second head

The names of the 199 workers who built the Eiffel Tower are engraved on the structure.

girder: a horizontal beam made of metal or wood used as a main support for a bridge or building

piece with the slightest defect rather than try to correct the problem on site.

With such meticulous preparation, the Eiffel Tower was not so much built as assembled from a kit. The construction crew consisted of about 200 workers divided into two teams. First, the assembly teams bolted the more than 15,000 metal girders into place. Then 20 teams of riveters replaced the bolts and hammered in permanent rivets—2.5 million in total.

Despite going to untested heights in construction, Alexandre Eiffel employed very little in the way of high-technology equipment. The only technical innovation he devised was a special "creeping crane." Four of these cranes moved vertically along the lift rails the workers built for the tower's elevator system to bring the metal pieces into position.

Under the watchful eyes of suspicious neighbors, the iron legs of the tower rose steadily into the sky. At 180 feet (55 meters), Eiffel connected the legs with an iron belt of trusses that formed the first platform. As the tower continued up to heights at which workers had never before operated, the crew began to balk. Twice they went on strike, demanding more pay for the risks they were taking. Although Eiffel pointed out that a worker would be just as dead from a fall at 300 feet (91 meters) as from one at 700 feet (213 meters), he gave in to the demands just enough to settle both strikes quickly.

As it turned out, the workers need not have worried. Eiffel maintained his spotless safety record. Not only were there no fatalities among the construction workers (although one worker died while installing an elevator after the tower was completed), there was not even a single accident involving dropped materials.

True to Eiffel's reputation, his crew completed the tower in March 1889, on time and under budget. After 635 days of work, the finished tower had reached its goal of 300 meters (984 feet).

The tower rose steadily in 1888. These views are dated January 7, June 19, and September 19.

In February 1889, the Eiffel Tower was almost complete.

THE RESULT

By the time the Eiffel Tower was finished, its breath-taking splendor had silenced most of its former critics. The building, which opened to the public on May 31, 1889, was the talk of the centennial celebration. During the 176 days of the exposition, almost 2 million visitors climbed or rode up into the iron tower to gain a view of a city's landscape "without its equal in the world."

Eiffel believed his tower represented the best of the industrial age. Beyond the fact that he had constructed a tower that surpassed any building ever attempted, he was most proud of the scientific purposes it served. Scientists used the unequaled height of the tower as a laboratory for studying wind, weather, and radio waves. The wind studies proved valuable in helping the French design aircraft propellers.

After reaching unmatched heights with his tall tower, Eiffel's career went into a tailspin. The engineer had signed a contract to build locks for the Panama Canal in the 1880s. When mismanagement and corruption torpedoed the French effort, Eiffel found himself caught in the crossfire. Although he had done nothing wrong, many French blamed him as one of the incompetent managers who wasted $287 million (1.5 billion francs) on the fiasco.

Eiffel spent much of his later life trying to clear his name. He largely succeeded, thanks in part to his great tower. His creation inspired a competition among French and English builders to outdo the Eiffel Tower, but none of their efforts succeeded.

When Eiffel died on December 27, 1923, more than 34 years after completing his great work, the Eiffel Tower was still the tallest human-made structure in the world. Six years later, the 1,046-foot (319-meter) Chrysler Building in New York City would be the first building to surpass it.

The tower is regularly inspected and receives a new coat of paint, known as Eiffel Tower brown, every seven years to prevent rust. The original elevator was replaced by four new ones in 1981, and the 1,290 ground spotlights that previously lit the tower have given way to illuminations along the girders. More than a century after the iron tower rose up in the skies above Paris, it remains the defining symbol of that great city.

Visitors board the elevator to the Eiffel Tower during the Universal Exposition of the Products of Industry in Paris in 1889.

CHAPTER FIVE

George W. Goethals and the Panama Canal

In January 1881, a French company confidently set off to tackle one of the most important engineering challenges in the world's history. This would be the fulfillment of a dream that dated back nearly 400 years to when Christopher Columbus tried to reach Asia by sailing west across the Atlantic Ocean. Columbus had stumbled upon a huge land mass that blocked the way. For centuries following that discovery, explorers vainly sought a passage through the Americas that would link the Atlantic and Pacific Oceans. The French believed they could create that link by digging a 47-mile long (75.7-kilometer) canal through a narrow section of Colombia known as the Isthmus of Panama.

The famous French diplomat Ferdinand de Lesseps had been recruited to lead the project. Twelve years earlier, de Lesseps had directed the construction of the Suez Canal. When he arrived in Panama, he declared that this new task of cutting a

The Gatun Upper Locks as they looked a few months before the Panama Canal opened for shipping in 1914. Army engineer George W. Goethals (1858-1928) considered the canal a mission from which there could be no retreat.

Diplomat and entrepreneur, Ferdinand de Lesseps (1805-1894) was decidedly not an engineer. He vastly underestimated the work required when he stated, "I maintain that Panama will be easier to make, easier to complete, and easier to keep up than Suez."

waterway through the mountains would be easier than digging in the Egyptian desert. He assured his investors that the job would take no more than seven years to complete. He was wrong.

At the rate the French were progressing in the mid-1880s, the project would have taken them a century to complete. The tropical climate and swampy terrain made Panama a deathtrap for construction workers. Smallpox, yellow fever, malaria, and cholera killed an estimated 2,000 French engineers and workers and more than 20,000 mostly Jamaican laborers. The project's chief engineer, Jules Dingler, returned home a broken man after his wife, son, and daughter all died in the Panamanian jungle.

After laboring nearly eight years under incredible hardships, de Lesseps's company abandoned Panama in disgrace. In addition to the loss of life, the company had squandered $287 million (1.5 billion francs). The 800,000 shareholders, most of whom were middle-class French families who had proudly invested their savings in their country, lost every franc. All they had to show for this sacrifice was a project less than one-tenth complete and a jungle full of rotting supplies and rusting equipment.

Fifteen years after the French gave up on the Panama Canal, the United States tried its luck with the project. After several lurching starts, the U.S. government turned to a no-nonsense army engineer, George Washington Goethals, to complete the gigantic task that de Lesseps had started.

Goethals was born in Brooklyn, New York, on June 29, 1858. He attended public schools in

In the 1850s, before the French began work on the canal, a group of American businessmen built a railroad across the Isthmus of Panama to transport travelers eager to reach the gold fields in California. The canal later followed basically the same route between the Atlantic and Pacific Oceans.

Brooklyn and Manhattan and then enrolled in the City College of New York at the age of 14. In 1876, he entered the U.S. Military Academy at West Point. Goethals never lost sight of the fact that all of these schools received support from government tax dollars. Later in his career, a private contractor offered him a huge increase in salary to retire from the army and join his firm. Goethals turned down the offer, saying, "All my training, all my education, has been at the expense of the public. . . . I owe it to the public to stay here."

Upon graduating second in his class from West Point in 1880, Goethals began slowly and quietly to build a solid record as an army engineer. First, he surveyed land in what was then the Washington Territory. Following his marriage to Effie Rodman in 1884, he joined an engineering team working on locks and dams along the Ohio River.

George Goethals showed such a mastery of engineering concepts that the army hired him to teach the subject at West Point in 1885. After four years in the classroom, Goethals was ready to return to field work. In 1890, he accepted responsibility for a major engineering project on the Cumberland and Tennessee Rivers. As part of this assignment, he designed and built a lock on the Tennessee River near Muscle Shoals, Alabama, capable of raising boats 26 feet (7.9 meters). This was a greater lift than any other engineer had ever achieved with a boat lock. Despite this accomplishment, Goethals remained unknown outside of the army.

Goethals was a shy man, which sometimes made him appear cold to those who worked with him. But he was a hard worker and an exceptional manager who knew how to delegate authority to his assistants. He also had the courage to take firm command when difficult occasions arose. While on assignment in Puerto Rico during the Spanish-American War in 1898, Goethals was ordered to build an emergency wharf. Unfortunately, there was no lumber available for the job. Rather than complaining about the situation, George Goethals acted boldly. Without permission, he took two barges captured from the Spanish and used them as a foundation for the wharf. That decision nearly brought

lock: a section of a waterway enclosed by gates in which boats are raised or lowered by raising or lowering the water level

court-martial charges from angry military officials. The only thing that mattered to Goethals, however, was that the wharf was built.

In 1900, Goethals began supervising construction of harbor defenses along the New England coast. Three years later, he returned to Washington to join the army's general staff with the rank of lieutenant colonel. While he was serving in this position, the United States sought to take over the failed French dream of building a canal through Panama. When Colombia balked at the terms of a treaty that would allow the United States to build the canal, President Theodore Roosevelt outmaneuvered the Colombian government by helping a group of Panamanians secede from Columbia on November 4, 1903. Then he negotiated a treaty with the new republic of Panama that allowed the U.S. to build and operate the canal.

Goethals traveled to Panama in 1905 as part of a government inspection tour. He showed little interest in the project except to register dismay at the organizational shambles under the first supervisor, John Findley Wallace. Roosevelt recruited John Frank "Big Smoke" Stevens, an engineer who had helped James J. Hill build his railroad empire and was currently vice president of the Chicago, Rock Island, & Pacific Railroad. But in early 1907, after only 18 months on the job, Stevens abruptly resigned. Fed up with unreliable civilian engineers, Roosevelt assigned control of the canal project to the best army engineer he could find—Colonel George W. Goethals.

In a 1911 speech, Theodore Roosevelt admitted, "I took the Isthmus, started the canal, and then left Congress not to debate the canal, but to debate me. . . . But while the debate goes on the canal does too."

John Stevens earned the nickname "Big Smoke" because of the big cigars he smoked and his forceful character. He never revealed his reasons for resigning, saying only they "were purely personal."

William C. Gorgas had survived yellow fever and was, therefore, immune to the disease when he arrived in Panama. He later served as U.S. surgeon general from 1914 to 1919.

When Goethals arrived in Panama, he found that a great deal had been accomplished in the time since he had toured the canal site. The most important work was that of the chief medical officer, Dr. William Gorgas, who had recognized the mosquito as the chief villain in most of Panama's health problems. Many canal officials scoffed at Gorgas's fixation on mosquitoes, and the doctor had experienced great difficulty in getting the supplies and cooperation he needed from Wallace. But Stevens had helped Gorgas push through his program of draining swamps, fumigating houses, installing screens on windows, and pouring "larvicide oil"—a chemical mixture that covered water with a film—on stagnant pools to prevent mosquitoes from breeding.

Gorgas's success was astounding. When he started his mosquito control effort, 65 workers died of yellow fever in a single month. Had this tragic death rate continued, the canal could never have been completed. But within six months, Gorgas virtually eliminated yellow fever from the Canal Zone. Malaria remained a problem, although mosquito control and daily doses of quinine reduced the number of cases.

Big Smoke Stevens had also accomplished much. Perhaps the most important decision he made was to abandon de Lesseps's notion of a sea-level canal. Stevens believed that cutting a canal at sea level through the mountainous ridge in central Panama was hopeless. Instead, he proposed using locks and dams to gradually raise and lower ships over the interior highlands, and he persuaded Congress to approve his plan.

John Stevens had also provided decent living conditions for the work force and reorganized the railways that became central to the operation. Trains removed dirt and transported workers, equipment, and supplies. George Goethals generously gave credit to the man he replaced. "The real problem in digging the canal has been the disposal of soil," reported Goethals, "and no army engineer in America could have laid out the transportation scheme as Stevens did."

Nonetheless, a project of such overwhelming size needed the firm guiding hand of one director who would keep moving forward in the face of daunting obstacles and who could coordinate thousands of small jobs so they would all come together in a single magnificent canal. Goethals was, in the words of one historian, "the right man in the right job at the right time."

While he was never as popular as the colorful Big Smoke Stevens, Goethals won the workers' respect. They found him humane and willing to listen. In a bold innovation in employee relations, Goethals set aside every Sunday morning from 7:30 until noon for his employees. Even when the work force swelled to 45,000, including people from 97 countries, he invited any employee with a complaint to bring it personally before him at this time. Goethals's smooth handling of his work force defused a potentially disastrous desertion that would have delayed, if not halted, the U.S. canal effort.

Of the 45,000 canal workers, only about 5,600 were Americans. Another 4,000 or so came from Europe. The majority, about 34,000, were West Indians from Barbados and Jamaica. Americans were called "gold employees" because their salaries were paid with American gold dollars. The rest of the workers were paid in Panamanian silver and called "silver employees." Gold employees earned more money, enjoyed better housing, and even had separate stores. Despite the unfair treatment and harsh working conditions, laborers continued to seek work on the canal because they could earn more money there than at home.

THE BREAKTHROUGH

Turning to the task at hand, Goethals faced two immediate problems. One was how to control the Chagres River. Engineers had selected this river basin as the best path for a canal across Panama. But because of torrential tropical rainfall that averaged between 130 and 150 inches (330 and 381 centimeters) per year, this river frequently flooded. Waters that could rise as much as 25 feet (7.6 meters) in a single night threatened to wash out any progress made in digging out the canal.

A second problem was where to dispose of the huge amount of earth from the excavation. By the time the canal was finished, workers would remove enough soil and rubble to cover New York's Manhattan Island 12 feet (3.7 meters) deep. No matter where they put it, the heavy rains seemed likely to wash it back into the river valley.

Goethals solved both problems with one solution: dams constructed partly from the excavated earth. "It is not so much a canal we are hoping to build as a bridge of water consisting of lakes, locks and sea-approaches," explained Goethals. "The rivers which flow into the Atlantic and Pacific are to be dammed back so that they form lakes . . . and these lakes will then be connected through the lowest point in the mountains by a deep cut."

In constructing the dam on the Pacific side, Goethals ran into the opposite problem. After the rocks used to form the dam's foundation sunk into the mud as fast as his workers could dump them, he

dam: a wall or barrier built across a river to control the flow of water. Water held back can be used for drinking, irrigation, or to power electric plants. Dams can be made of earth and rock or of concrete.

ordered new soundings made. To his horror, they found "blue clay without grit, possessing but little supporting power." The mud was 70 feet (21.3 meters) deep, not 10 feet (3.1 meters) as previous reports had indicated. Goethals knew that if he proposed moving the dam, canal critics would hoot at the mistake. Nonetheless, he refused to compromise on safety and instead insisted on moving the dam and two locks more than four miles (six kilometers) inland to Miraflores. Fortunately, Roosevelt approved the change, the press ignored the story, and the Panama Canal inched forward.

The diversions and dams held back the river waters while Goethals turned loose the steam shovels to carve the canal into the interior of Panama. He frowned on the competition among the workers

Although the Panama Canal connects east and west sections of the world, it actually runs northwest to southeast across Panama. The Gatun, Pedro Miguel, and Miraflores Locks raise or lower ships to the level of Gatun Lake, which is 85 feet (25.9 meters) higher than the Atlantic Ocean and 24 miles (38.6 kilometers) across.

In November 1906, when Theodore Roosevelt traveled to Panama to view the construction, he became the first president of the United States to travel outside of the country while holding office.

to break individual records for the amount of dirt and rock loosened, scooped up, and carried away. Goethals did not want workers wearing out the equipment through overuse. But he coordinated the efforts of so many workers and so much machinery that his team moved more dirt in a single day than previous French and American teams had moved in months.

The most difficult digging project was cutting through the Culebra Pass at the south end of Gatun Lake. Even though Goethals would be using locks to lift ships 85 feet (25.9 meters) in elevation, he still needed to blast an 8.5-mile-long (13.7-kilometer) and 45-foot-deep (13.7-meter) gap through this mountain in order to complete the canal. Gouging an opening through this mountain pass was especially difficult because the mountains were partially composed of slick clay. When rocks were dug or blasted out, the entire unstable hillside often collapsed. In a few minutes, a slide could wipe out the progress of weeks of backbreaking labor.

Goethals had not been in Panama six months before a mudslide smashed and buried trains, tracks, and shovels. Throughout his years in Panama, the shifting and sliding rocks of Culebra battered Goethals's crew relentlessly. Every time the 6,000 men working on the Culebra Cut seemed to be making progress, another wall of dirt would cave in. The 22 major landslides that Goethals faced made the digging as frustrating as trying to empty the ocean with buckets. In 1906, an international board of engineers had calculated that the United States would need to dig out 500,000 cubic yards (380,000 cubic meters) of dirt to complete the job. Largely because of the slides, within two years, U.S. engineers revised the estimate to 78 million cubic yards (59 million cubic meters). Even that proved to be far short of the final mark—it is estimated that 232,440,945 cubic yards (104,598,450 cubic meters) of dirt were removed.

But unlike those who preceded him, Goethals saw the building of the canal as a mission from which there was no possibility of retreat. "I consider that I am commander of the Army of Panama," he

Trains and steam shovels as well as a portion of the canal bed were buried in this Culebra mudslide in November 1909.

declared, "and that the enemy we are going to combat is the Culebra Cut and the locks and dams at both ends of the canal."

Goethals's cool determination kept the crew going in times of emergency. In 1913, when the canal was nearing completion, the most devastating landslide yet occurred in Culebra Pass. Goethals rushed to the spot of the slide and found the supervisor, Major David Gaillard, in shock. The pass on which the crew had worked so hard for over six years lay smothered under a landslide.

"What are we going to do now?" Gaillard cried in despair.

Unflappable as always, Goethals said simply, "Dig it out again."

Hundreds of men died in rock slides, machine or dynamite accidents, and drownings, as well as from heat exhaustion, while trying to open the Culebra Pass. Finally, after seven years of constant effort and 61 million pounds (28 million kilograms) of dynamite, the great job was completed.

While digging out a trench through the mountains, Goethals's other main task was constructing locks far larger than any ever imagined. Plans called for 6 pairs of locks with concrete floors up to 20 feet (6.1 meters) thick. The walls at the bottom of each lock would be 50 feet (15.2 meters) thick, tapering off to a width of 8 feet (2.4 meters) on top. Each of these locks had to be long enough and wide enough to accommodate the largest ships that engineers could envision: 1,000 feet long, 110 feet wide, and 80 feet deep (305 by 33.5 meters and 24.4 meters deep).

I was his assistant for seven years, and I might say that everything in my life since has seemed comparatively easy.
—Lt. Robert Wood, describing Col. George W. Goethals

Each day for two solid years, Goethals's engineers mixed and poured twice as much concrete as any crew had ever managed before in a single day. Under his direction, the locks were finished in four years—right on schedule. They were designed with culverts, or drains, 18 feet (5.5 meters) in diameter with 100 holes that allowed water to seep in smoothly. When ships needed to be raised up to the level of the highlands, water flowed through the holes and filled the lock. When ships needed to be

The Gatun Upper Locks, shown above as they looked in July 1910, were designed to accommodate the largest ship imaginable at the time. The Titanic *could have fit through these locks and the canal if it had not sunk in 1912.*

lowered back to sea level, pumps drained water from the locks. Mammoth metal doors, called miter gates, held the water inside the locks while the ships were raised and lowered.

Since ships could not maneuver through the narrow locks, Goethals installed electric trams—cars that run on tracks—to do the job. These "mules," as they were nicknamed, towed the ships through the locks with steel cables. The mules were powered by the hydroelectric plant Goethals had built by the Gatun Dam.

No one had ever constructed a series of locks on such an enormous scale before, and no one had ever tried electric mules to tow such huge ships as would come through the canal. As workers prepared to open the canal for business, tensions ran high. After the incredible expense and labor, what if the locks and dams did not work? Goethals's worst fears nearly came true two weeks before the scheduled official opening of the canal. While testing the pulling ability of the electric mules on the *Cristobal*, a cable snapped, and the ship nearly collided with a lock.

But on Saturday morning, August 15, 1914, the dredge ship *Ancon* entered the canal system from the Atlantic Ocean. All locks worked to perfection. Nine hours later, the *Ancon* reached the Pacific port of Balboa. Thirty-three years after the French had begun the digging, the Panama Canal finally opened for business.

Shortly after the Panama Canal opened for shipping, the New York Times *wrote, "The construction of the Panama Canal by the Army engineers has added more to the fame of this country among civilized nations than any of its achievements since the founding of the government."*

THE RESULT

The immediate impact of the Panama Canal was to shave weeks off the length of many ocean voyages. Prior to the canal's construction, a ship traveling between New York and San Francisco had to sail all the way around the southern tip of South America—a distance of some 13,000 miles (20,930 kilometers). Thanks to the 47-mile (76-kilometer) shortcut through Panama, sailors could reduce the distance to 5,000 miles (8,050 kilometers). Between 12,000 and 15,000 ships pass through the canal's locks each year, saving an estimated 120 million miles (193 million kilometers) of ocean travel.

Not only did this shortcut save time and money for commercial shipping, it also provided a strategic boost to the United States military forces. Prior to the building of the canal, if war broke out in either the Pacific or Atlantic Oceans, many weeks would pass before reinforcements from the other ocean could sail around South America. The Panama Canal greatly strengthened the U.S. military by allowing the navy to move ships quickly from one ocean to the other. This advantage led Theodore Roosevelt to declare that the Panama Canal ranked with the Louisiana Purchase as the two most important peacetime events in the nation's history.

The building of the canal also helped establish the United States as the dominant economic power in the world. Although Goethals modestly insisted that the construction of the Panama Canal was not a difficult technological challenge, he had performed

Columbia, Harvard, and Yale Universities all awarded George Goethals honorary degrees for his accomplishment. Teddy Roosevelt wrote, "Colonel Goethals proved to be the man of all others to do the job. It would be impossible to overstate what he has done."

George Goethals, in turn, wrote, "The real builder of the canal was Theodore Roosevelt. It could not have been more of a personal triumph if he had personally lifted every shovelful of earth in its construction."

an astounding feat. Even Big Smoke Stevens, who had little to say about the canal after his mysterious resignation, commented, "The work of Goethals . . . was, in my judgment, above just criticism." The U.S. government rewarded Goethals by promoting him to major general in 1915 and appointing him the first governor of the Canal Zone.

Goethals completed a construction project on a scale vastly beyond what any nation had ever achieved. The feeling emerged among American engineers that if Goethals could build a huge canal through the swampy jungles of Panama, there was nothing other engineers could not accomplish.

Although not as militarily important today, the Panama Canal is still heavily traveled. It is also still under construction. The Culebra Cut, renamed the Gaillard Cut after the engineer in charge of the digging there, is being widened from 500 to 630 feet (152 to 192 meters) along straight stretches and to 730 feet (223 meters) at curves to meet shipping demands and permit two-way traffic. This project is scheduled to be finished in 2002, but the cut will always require continuous dredging.

Since the 1977 Torrijos-Carter treaty between the United States and the republic of Panama, the U.S. has gradually transferred full responsibility for operating, administering, and governing the Canal Zone to Panama. The treaty also guarantees the canal will remain "open, safe, neutral and accessible to vessels of all nations."

dredge: to deepen harbors and waterways with a machine or boat equipped with scooping or suction devices

CHAPTER SIX

Frank Crowe
and the Hoover Dam

In 1928, the United States Congress passed legislation that would change the entire landscape of the Southwest. Congress authorized the building of the Boulder Dam, later renamed the Hoover Dam, which was to be the key link in harnessing the water of the Colorado River to bring much-needed water and electricity to the growing number of people living in the deserts and valleys of southern California. Plans called for the construction of a huge dam in one of the hottest canyons in North America, in an area so rugged and remote that no roads existed within dozens of miles of the place.

For those engineers experienced in building dams, the plan sounded like the worst nightmare ever devised for their profession. Yet virtually every civil engineer in the United States dreamed of landing the job. No one doubted that the Hoover Dam would provide the ultimate challenge in dam construction.

One of the men who worked for Frank Crowe (1882-1946) described him as both an engineering genius and a genius at managing people. The Hoover Dam was his masterpiece.

It was only fitting that the honor of building the legendary dam should go to a legendary engineer—Frank Crowe. Francis T. "Frank" Crowe, born in 1882 in Trenholmville, Quebec, was the son of an English woolen mill operator who immigrated to North America in 1869. Frank spent most of his childhood in New England. Like Marc Brunel, Frank came under a great deal of pressure from his father to enter the ministry. But his love of science and mathematics was so obvious that his father relented and allowed him to pursue his chosen career. In 1901, Frank enrolled at the University of Maine to study civil engineering.

During his junior year at college, Crowe heard Frank Weymouth deliver a lecture describing his work with the United States Bureau of Reclamation. Weymouth was helping to dam rivers in the western states as part of a federal government effort to provide irrigation for farmers in that dry region. The lure of the wide open West was more than Crowe could resist. He went up to Weymouth after the lecture and asked him for a summer job.

Crowe's boldness worked. That summer, Crowe joined a reclamation crew performing a survey of the drainage basin of the Yellowstone River in Montana. He so enjoyed working in the scenic wilderness that when the summer was over, he could hardly wait to get back to it. When he graduated from the University of Maine in 1905, he skipped his graduation ceremony and took the first train west.

Skilled field engineers were in great demand in the West, and Crowe had no difficulty finding work.

For the next two decades, he worked on a variety of construction projects in remote areas of Montana, Wyoming, and Idaho. He became obsessed with getting work done faster and more efficiently and thought about it even while he and his wife, Linnie, traveled to New York City on their honeymoon. According to Linnie, the highlight of their tour of the city for Frank was watching a new type of automatic dump truck rapidly unload coal through a small chute without spilling.

In every construction project, Crowe tried out new techniques and designed new equipment to dig and move earth faster. He became especially good at constructing the gigantic concrete dams that the government authorized to tame western rivers. Two of his pioneering methods helped make these challenging engineering projects more practical. First, he organized trucks and trains into an efficient delivery system that could move massive amounts of concrete to the construction site rapidly. Then he developed an overhead cable and grid system for quickly bringing small loads of concrete to the exact spot where they were needed.

Crowe's success won him rapid promotions. After only six years on the job, he advanced to the position of assistant superintendent of the Arrowrock Dam project on the Boise River in Idaho. Before long, he was supervising his own dam projects. By the time he completed the Tieton Dam near Yakima, Washington, in 1924, he stood unchallenged as the government's outstanding field engineer. The government rewarded him by appointing him general

Frank Crowe's problem-solving skills were legendary. According to his old mentor, Frank Weymouth, "Nothing stumps him. He finds a way out of every difficulty."

Work on projects such as the Arrowrock Dam on the Boise River in Idaho prepared Frank Crowe for bigger challenges.

superintendent of construction for the Bureau of Reclamation. This gave Crowe responsibility for overseeing all government field construction projects in 17 western states.

Unfortunately for Crowe, the federal government changed its policy on awarding contracts. Instead of having the Bureau of Reclamation perform the actual construction, the government decided to bid out the work to private contractors. That reduced Crowe's position to an administrative desk job. Crowe had not come out West to fill out forms and file reports. He bragged that he never in his life wrote anything longer than one page. If he could not be out on the construction sites, working alongside the crew, he did not want the job. After a brief time at his new post, Crowe resigned to join the Morrison-Knudsen Company, a private firm that bid on government dam projects.

While with Morrison-Knudsen, Frank Crowe directed construction on the Guernsey Dam on the North Platte River in Wyoming, the Coombe Dam along the Bear River in California, and the Deadwood Dam on the Deadwood River in Idaho. He completed all of these projects on time and under budget. These successes, however, were just warmups compared to the challenge that arose in the early 1930s.

For more than a decade, the U.S. government had planned an ambitious program to bring water to the vast tracts of dry land in the Southwest. The source for this water was the Colorado River, which flowed for 1,400 miles (2,254 kilometers) through some of the most arid land in North America before emptying into the Gulf of California. The federal government decided to siphon off some of this water by building a series of dams on the Colorado.

The most important link in this chain of dams was the Boulder Dam, on the Arizona and Nevada border. Actually, the dam was misnamed. Government engineers had originally expected to locate the dam in Boulder Canyon. But after Walker Young spent three years mapping, drilling, and surveying the rugged river and land in the early 1920s, the engineers decided to move the dam a short way to Black Canyon. The name Boulder Dam stuck with the project until the dam was renamed in 1947 to honor President Herbert Hoover.

Crowe could hardly have imagined a more daunting place to construct a dam. Black Canyon was deep and narrow, and located in rugged, remote wilderness. There were neither roads nor rail tracks to bring materials to the dam site. The nearest town, Las Vegas, Nevada, was 30 miles (48.3 kilometers) northwest of the dam site, in the middle of a desert. Working conditions would be deadly. Black Canyon's average high temperature in July was a scorching 119 degrees Fahrenheit (48 degrees Celsius), and it cooled off to about 95 degrees F (35 degrees C) at night. In these nearly impossible conditions, the plan was to construct the largest and highest dam in the world. Many respected engineers said the obstacles were too great; that the dam simply could not be built.

canyon: a narrow opening between steep cliff walls

Although he had supported building the Boulder Dam, naming the project after President Herbert Hoover (1874-1964) was not a popular idea. Many people blamed the economic hardships of the Great Depression on Hoover's policies.

THE BREAKTHROUGH

But to Frank Crowe, the Hoover Dam was the challenge of a lifetime. He had followed the progress of the dam plans for over a decade. Now that the government was ready to begin work on the project, Crowe admitted, "I was wild to build this dam . . . the biggest dam ever built by anyone anywhere."

In order to get the chance, Frank Crowe had to underbid several competitors on the project. This

The Black Canyon as it looked before construction of the Hoover Dam began

was risky because with all the hazards and unpredictable occurrences, he could only make a rough guess at how much the project would cost. Crowe took a huge gamble on his own skill as an engineer and offered to build the dam for $48,890,955, which was $5 million less than the bid of his closest competitor.

The project was so huge that Morrison-Knudsen had joined with five other construction companies in February 1931. The new entity, called Six Companies, had pooled their resources to submit the required $2 million bond with the bid. The only way Six Companies could avoid a disastrous financial loss on the project was if engineer Frank Crowe could build the dam faster and more efficiently than anyone else had dreamed possible.

Crowe could not hope to build the dam without attracting the best construction workers in the land. Here he had an advantage over his competitors. Every construction worker in the West knew of Crowe's reputation as the best in the business. Although Crowe worked his crews hard, he treated them fairly. Rather than sit back in an office and give orders, he was always on site with the crew. As a result, many of his workers followed him from project to project. Despite the terrible working conditions, these veteran workers answered his call to join him on the Hoover Dam project.

The pressure on Crowe was enormous from the start. In the 17 months since the stock market crashed in October 1929, unemployment was soaring in the United States. Rather than allow Crowe to spend time carefully laying the groundwork for the project, President Herbert Hoover insisted the project get underway immediately to provide much-needed jobs. Construction work began in March 1931, six months sooner than Crowe had planned. Thousands of desperate workers flocked to Las Vegas, which had a population of only 5,000 at the time, to find work. Crowe had to build roads and railroads, bring water and power sources to the site, and arrange transportation for the workers. At the same time, he was creating the entirely new town of Boulder City in the desert near the dam location. Here dormitories for single men and small cottages for families were hastily assembled.

The workers also had to be fed. The gigantic 1,150-seat mess hall was one of the many construction projects in Boulder City.

Crowe set his crews to work blasting roads, pathways, and loading areas out of the solid rock walls of the canyon. Using picks, jackhammers, and dynamite, they chiseled 21 miles (33.8 kilometers) of railroad track through mountains of rock to provide access around the remote dam site. As usual, Crowe set up an efficient system that made the best use of all his workers. Whereas all previous major construction projects in the West had used horses for transportation in remote areas, he saw this as a job for machines. Crowe brought bigger and better trucks, generators, and power shovels into the work area than had ever been used before. Reclamation Commissioner Elwood Mead marveled, "Those western dirt-moving fools are building highways, starting tunnels, and laying railroad all at once, but without any mixups."

There was no way a dam could be constructed while the Colorado flowed through the canyon. The riverbed needed to be absolutely dry before the work could begin, so Crowe had to find a way to divert the mighty river for the four years it would take to build the dam. This proved to be the most difficult task of the project. The steep rock canyon allowed no alternative route for the water to flow, so Crowe's crews had to blast tunnels through the canyon walls to carry the river around the dam site.

They began by floating equipment down the river on barges to a point upriver from the dam site. Since there was no level area on which to set up operations, they first had to dig and scrape out a landing area for the equipment.

Then, in late June 1931, came the work of gouging out four tunnels through solid rock, each 56 feet (17.1 meters) in diameter and between 3,500 and 4,000 feet (1,067 and 1,219 meters) long. Miners worked on a huge motorized rig they called a "jumbo," which was equipped with 30 rock drills. They would drill holes, fit the holes with dynamite, then back out of the tunnel and blast. Workers removed the debris and then the jumbos moved back into the tunnel to repeat the process.

One of the "jumbos" used to carve out the four diversion tunnels

Always a fanatic about getting the job done on time, Crowe sometimes sacrificed safety in the name of speed. While he introduced some safety innovations—his crews were among the first to use hard hats to protect their heads from falling rocks and tools—he ignored other safety procedures that could have saved lives. For example, the air in the tunnels was like an oven. It heated up to as much as 130 degrees F (54 degrees C) during the day and, with little ventilation in the shafts, it did not cool down much at night. Crowe made no serious efforts to protect the workers from the effects of the heat.

Crowe also ignored Nevada mining safety regulations that banned the use of gasoline engines in poorly ventilated tunnels and mines because the engines emit carbon monoxide, a deadly poisonous gas that has no odor or color. Instead of using safer electric-powered trams, Crowe continued to use trucks to carry out the waste material. During the more than five years of construction, there would be more than 100 deaths—not only from heat and carbon monoxide, but also from rock slides, falls, electrocution, and drowning.

Crowe put 1,500 men to work on the tunnels. In early February 1932, they finished carving out the massive holes. Now they needed to smooth the inside of the tunnels and reinforce them with a three-inch-thick (7.6 centimeter) lining of concrete. Before they could get started on this, though, a freak flash flood raged through the canyon and into the tunnels. Construction workers spent a week removing the sludge from the flood.

In a single summer month of 1931, heat in the tunnels claimed the lives of 14 workers. The following summer, a team of scientists from Harvard University arrived to study the situation. They identified **dehydration**, or lack of water, as the problem. Once workers were provided with plenty of drinking water and encouraged to salt their food, the deaths due to the heat decreased.

ventilation: the process of circulating fresh air into a building or other place. Vent comes from a Latin word meaning "wind."

Once, while the late-night crew was pouring concrete into forms for the tunnel lining, the foreman and his crew began arguing about whether they had filled the forms full enough. Suddenly a voice out of the darkness boomed, "Who is holding up this pour?" It was Crowe. Although it was 3 A.M., he was on the job, fretting as always about wasted seconds.

Crowe balanced his hard-driving discipline with a sharp sense of humor. At an important business conference held in the company mess hall, he stepped forward to introduce the main speaker, Nevada senator Key Pittman. Just then, there was a tremendous crash in the kitchen as a pile of dishes fell to the floor. In the moment of silence that followed, the entire gathering heard Harold Anderson, the head of food service, cursing loudly in the kitchen. "I was supposed to give the first speech," Crowe quipped, "but Harold just beat me to it."

As hard as he drove his men, Crowe drove himself even harder. He lost 27 pounds (12.2 kilograms) from spending every day in the heat of the tunnels and the canyons. Many of the crew wondered if he ever slept.

When the concrete lining was finished, crews began dumping muck across the Colorado to divert the river into the tunnels. They had to build the temporary dam so solid and high that the river would not seep into the dam construction site even during one of its infamous spring flood rampages. Crowe put 3,400 workers on the job.

Crowe had ordered an enormous concrete mixing plant erected near the construction site while the tunnels and temporary dam were being built. Construction experts commented that the plant, the railroad tracks built into the canyon, and the diversion tunnels were each, by themselves, incredible feats of engineering. Yet Crowe had to construct all of these before he could even start the main task of constructing the dam.

Once the Colorado River was safely diverted in November 1932, the crews began digging the riverbed down to bedrock so they would have a solid foundation on which to anchor the dam. Trucks hauled out the silt and gravel and deposited it in railroad cars to be carried away. The crews answered Crowe's relentless quest for speed. One crew loaded up 1,841 trucks in an eight-hour shift—an average of nearly one every four minutes. In mid-April 1933, they finally struck bedrock 40 feet (12.2 meters) below the river level.

Two months later, the crew was at last ready to begin construction of the dam itself. Constructing a dam, however, was not a simple matter of pouring concrete. Crowe and his engineers calculated that if they poured concrete into a single giant frame, the pressure and interactions of materials would cause the temperature of the concrete to rise by 40 degrees Fahrenheit (22 degrees Celsius). It would then take 125 years for the concrete to cool sufficiently to harden! Even then, the concrete would not cool at an even rate throughout the entire dam, and severe cracks would form.

Crowe's answer was to pour the concrete in individual blocks no more than five feet (1.5 meters) thick. They were set upon one another like a pile of boxes. Meanwhile, he decided to run a network of 1-inch (2.54-centimeter) pipes through the blocks. These pipes would carry water from the Colorado River to cool the concrete evenly. In his insatiable desire for efficiency, Crowe later sped up the cooling process by refrigerating the water.

The first buckets of concrete were ready on June 6, 1933. It was through his ingenious method of concrete pouring that Frank Crowe made the project economically profitable for Six Companies. Improving on the system he introduced in 1911 at Arrowrock, he had steel cables strung between 90-foot (27.4-meter) towers that moved up and down the river on railroad tracks. The cables created a massive web of wires. Crews could maneuver buckets of concrete along this web to whisk the concrete to exactly the right location in a matter of seconds.

During the summer of 1934, workers pour concrete into the many blocks that form the dam. There is enough concrete in the Hoover Dam to pave a highway 16 feet (5 meters) wide from New York City to San Francisco.

agitator: a tool or machine that shakes or stirs a substance

Crowe also introduced a new type of portable agitator to keep the concrete from hardening while it was transported to the most inaccessible corners of the canyon.

There were dangers involved with Crowe's high-wire delivery system. Cables snapped every so often, sending buckets crashing into the workers below. But overall, the coordination was masterful.

Crowe had figured out a way to keep 5,000 crew members actively at work in the cramped space of a narrow canyon. Concrete flowed into the Black Canyon at an unheard-of rate. In March 1934, the crew poured an astounding 1,100 8-ton (7.3-metric ton) buckets of concrete in one day.

Crowe's delivery system rocketed the project far ahead of schedule. The original bid had called for the crew to begin pouring concrete in early December 1934. Instead, they were almost finished with the pour by that date. In February 1935, all the concrete was in place and curing. Workers permanently sealed the two inner tunnels, numbers two and three. Tunnel one was fitted with a concrete plug perforated with 6-foot (1.8-meter) diameter holes that could be opened or closed as water was needed to irrigate farms in the Imperial Valley of California. A steel gate was then placed in front of the fourth tunnel and the Colorado River, now harnessed, was returned to its original course.

A reservoir of water, Lake Mead, formed behind the dam. During the summer of 1935, a reduced work force constructed the powerhouse that would convert the water power of the river into electricity for southern California, Nevada, and Arizona. President Franklin D. Roosevelt dedicated the structure on September 30, 1935. Five months later, Six Companies officially terminated their contract with the government. The Bureau of Reclamation supervised the installation of generators in the powerhouse that produce electricity.

The huge reservoir created by the Hoover Dam was named Lake Mead to honor Bureau of Reclamation Commissioner Elwood Mead, who died in 1936. Mead had been a strong advocate of the dam during both the Hoover and Roosevelt administrations.

Over 100 workers died building the Hoover Dam. The first fatality was J. G. Tierney, U.S. Bureau of Reclamation, who drowned while surveying the river on December 20, 1922. In a sad twist of fate, his son, Patrick W. Tierney, fell from an intake tower on the same date 13 years later and became the last to die on the project.

THE RESULT

Frank Crowe not only completed a difficult assignment, he finished it two years ahead of schedule and under budget. The speed with which he constructed the dam earned Six Companies a 25 percent profit and his own personal fortune. The completion of his crowning achievement, however, plunged Crowe into a depression. After throwing his heart and soul into the greatest engineering project ever, Crowe suddenly found himself without any challenges. He knew he would never have the chance to build a dam the equal of Hoover.

Frank Crowe continued to build dams, including the giant Shasta Dam in northern California. But the enthusiasm was no longer there. After finishing the Shasta Dam in 1944, he retired to a cattle ranch in Redding, California. Ill-suited to a life of leisure, he died there on February 26, 1946.

The Hoover Dam remains a breathtaking engineering feat that continues to amaze visitors to the Southwest. Built in a remote, hostile environment, it towers 726 feet (221.3 meters) high over a rugged, scenic canyon. The dam contains 4.5 million cubic yards (3.4 million cubic meters) of concrete—more than was used in all Bureau of Reclamation dams before 1931 combined.

In sheer size, however, other dams have since surpassed the Hoover Dam. The Grand Coulee Dam on the Columbia River in Washington, completed in 1941, held the title of the largest concrete construction of any kind for half a century. But the

Obituaries described Crowe's long and distinguished career in heavy construction. . . . Eulogists in Las Vegas and Boulder City spoke of his devotion to family, friends, and protégés, of his fairmindedness, of his sense of humor, and of his absolute integrity. But in the end Frank Crowe was remembered for one thing: he was the man who built Hoover Dam. Those closest to him knew that he had never hoped for anything more.

—Joseph Stevens, author of *Hoover Dam: An American Adventure*

difficulty of construction, the unforgiving environment, and the innovative techniques used make the Hoover Dam perhaps the most famous dam ever built. It stands today as an important landmark in American history as well as in engineering. It is the main link in a chain of dams that helped open up the arid lands of the Southwest to development, thereby allowing southern California to become one of the most populated regions in the country. The state of Arizona has also seen huge growth in agriculture and population.

The Hoover Dam and the lake it created have become popular tourist destinations. So has Las Vegas. Once a small western town (population 5,000 in 1930), it is now a gambling and entertainment center that is home to over 436,000 people and many millions of visitors every year.

Engineer Frank Crowe (far right) escorts visitors viewing progress of the Hoover Dam.

CHAPTER SEVEN

William Lamb and the Empire State Building

Prior to the 1890s, there was no such thing as a skyline in the major cities of the world. The tallest buildings rarely stood more than six stories above the ground. For reasons of safety, convenience, and cost, architects could not plan anything higher. No one wanted to have to climb more than six flights of stairs on a regular basis, and elevators were risky because the cables holding the cars or platforms sometimes broke. Even if builders could get around these problems, a high-rise building required a wide base and massive walls to support the weight piled on top of it.

But by the late 1800s, these obstacles to high-rise building had fallen. In 1853, Elisha Otis's elevator introduced a spring-latch that jammed into a rail to prevent an elevator from falling even if the cables broke. Then, in the 1880s, engineers found they could use steel frames to support the weight of a building.

Architect William Lamb (1883-1952) said his design for the Empire State Building was determined by simple, logical answers to economic demands.

113

A **skyscraper** is a tall building constructed on a steel skeleton with elevators to transport people from floor to floor. Early skyscrapers were about 10 stories tall; later ones rose 100 stories or more.

The Flatiron Building is New York City's oldest skyscraper. Originally named the Fuller Building, its unique wedge shape reminded people of an ordinary household clothes iron.

Freed from the old restrictions, architects and engineers created the skyscraper, which architect Harvey Wiley Corbett called the first new structural form since the ancient Romans invented the arch. The race to the sky was on!

Chicago was the first city in which 10-story skyscrapers loomed over the city streets. But skyscraper fever soon infected builders in New York City. With prices for real estate in the business districts soaring, New York developers saw they could save money by building tall buildings on small plots of land. Along with this practical consideration, the spirit of competition fueled one grand building scheme after another. Many wealthy New Yorkers cherished the dream of owning the world's tallest building.

In 1903, the 20-story Flatiron Building brought the honor of having the world's tallest building to New York City. Ten years later, dime-store wizard F. W. Woolworth surpassed the Flatiron's claim to fame with the construction of a daring 60-story, 792-foot (241-meter) building. For more than 15 years, no one challenged the Woolworth Building's reign as king of the skyscrapers. But, like a magical forest, buildings rose into the skyline of New York City at an astounding rate. By 1929, the city had 2,479 skyscrapers, 188 of which stood higher than the old Flatiron Building.

In that year, several prominent business groups took aim at Woolworth's title. A furious three-way race to construct the world's tallest building led to the creation of the Empire State Building. Not only did it capture bragging rights for its investors, but it won lasting recognition as the most majestic skyscraper ever built. Surprisingly, the man most responsible for its design was neither a well-known architect nor a visionary artist. Most of his peers did not even think of him as particularly creative, and he never designed another noteworthy building.

His name was William F. Lamb, a man of Scottish descent who was born in Brooklyn, New York, on November 21, 1883. The son of a builder, Lamb stuck to the safe and familiar rather than seeking adventurous challenges. He followed his father into the field of construction. After graduating in 1904 from Williams College, Williamstown, Massachusetts, he pursued graduate work in architecture at Columbia University in New York City. He also attended the prestigious École des Beaux Arts in Paris.

After earning an advanced degree in architecture from the French school, Lamb returned to New York in 1911 and joined the architectural firm of Carrère and Hastings. John M. Carrère was killed in an auto accident a few months after Lamb signed on with the company. The surviving partner, Thomas Hastings, gradually lost interest in his work. This sudden loss of leadership allowed two young associates, Lamb and R. H. Shreve, to assume more and more responsibility. When Hastings retired in 1920, Shreve and Lamb were ready and willing to take charge of the highly respected architectural firm. The two young partners capitalized on the Carrère and Hastings name for several years before

The elevators invented by Elisha Graves Otis (1811-1861) made building skyscrapers practical.

Frank Winfield Woolworth (1852-1919) revolutionized retail merchandising and then used his fortune to build a skyscraper that held the title of the world's tallest building from 1913 to 1930.

Richmond H. Shreve graduated from Cornell College of Architecture in 1902 and joined the faculty there. During his four years of teaching, he supervised construction of Goldwin Smith Hall, which was built by Carrère and Hastings, the firm he later joined.

they established themselves well enough to change the name to Shreve & Lamb in 1925.

The partners had skills that complemented each other perfectly. Richmond H. Shreve was a skilled organizer with a knack for working out detailed production schedules; William Lamb preferred to work on design problems. Together, the two developed a reputation as practical, solid, no-frills architects who completed their work on time. Their approach appealed to many businessmen, who often grew frustrated with architects who wanted to build splashy or innovative buildings without regard to the cost. When Lamb declared, "The day that an architect could sit by his drawing board and make pretty sketches of decidedly uneconomical monuments to himself is gone," cost-conscious executives applauded. Here was an architect who understood that the main function of a business was to make a profit. When they hired Shreve & Lamb, clients knew they might not end up with a work of art, but they were going to get the most building at the lowest price.

In 1928, Shreve and Lamb landed their most important contract to date—designing the General Motors Building. This put them in contact with one of General Motors' top executives, John Jacob Raskob. Raskob had lived in poverty all his life until he landed a job in 1900 as a bookkeeper for Pierre Du Pont, one of the nation's wealthiest men. He so impressed Du Pont with his financial expertise that his boss made him his personal secretary. It was Raskob who steered Du Pont into investing in

General Motors stock. When General Motors became a successful automobile manufacturer in the 1920s, Du Pont made millions on the deal. Raskob also earned himself a fortune. Perhaps more importantly, Raskob's financial skills were noticed by General Motors executives, and he was given the position of chairman of finance at the company.

Raskob thought he could make money by constructing a large office building in New York City and then renting it out to tenants. Given the price of real estate, he wanted a tall skyscraper to give him the most office space at the least cost. At the same time, the notion of being master of the world's tallest building appealed to him. John Raskob was not interested in style or innovation; instead he wanted a tall, economical building that would help him turn a profit. His accountants told him that in order to make the investment a success, he needed to start collecting rent from tenants within two years after the project was launched. The General Motors Building that Shreve & Lamb had just designed for Raskob and brought to completion within a tight deadline was the kind of plain, practical building he needed. He knew he could count on them to design something along the same lines for his new project.

When Raskob approached Shreve, Lamb, and Arthur Loomis Harmon (who had joined the firm in 1929 as a third partner) with his proposal, the architects wondered if the man knew what he was asking. Raskob wanted the world's tallest building, and he wanted it finished in less than two years.

John Jacob Raskob (1879-1950) was involved in politics as well as business. When his friend, Alfred E. Smith, received the presidential nomination from the Democratic Party in 1928, Raskob resigned from GM to become National Chairman of the Democratic Party. Smith lost but later became president of the company Raskob created to build the Empire State Building.

The previous year, that would have meant a structure over 60 stories, or about 800 feet (244 meters). But the competition had suddenly grown fierce. In 1929, the Bank of Manhattan and the Chrysler Corporation both began constructing buildings that dwarfed the Woolworth Building. At 925 feet (282 meters), the Bank of Manhattan was to be slightly higher than the Chrysler Building. But Chrysler trumped its rival by making a last-minute revision of plans that raised its building to 967 feet (295 meters).

That meant that Raskob's building, which he called the Empire State Building, would have to be roughly 1,000 feet (305 meters) high. All that height would have to fit on the small 200- by 400-foot (61- by 122-meter) site that Raskob had purchased on Fifth Avenue between 33rd and 34th Streets. The famous Waldorf-Astoria luxury hotel, opened in 1893, stood on the lot. But the elegant hotel was no longer in style or profitable, and the owners were willing to sell.

Furthermore, the architects would have to work around the city's strict building code for this area of Fifth Avenue. Buildings there were prohibited from rising more than 125 feet (38 meters), or about 12 stories straight up from the ground. In order to comply with the code, Raskob's building would have to be recessed as it went up.

The Waldorf-Astoria was the city's largest and most prestigious hotel when it opened in the 1890s. In 1929, it was torn down to make room for the Empire State Building.

THE BREAKTHROUGH

Lamb realized that although the demands were great, perhaps even impossible, this was a unique chance to create something historic. After mulling over the project, he agreed to take it, with one uncharacteristic condition: the building had to be beautiful. Raskob told him to do what he wished as long as he met the deadline and the budget.

Raskob's grand plan nearly had to be scrapped. Shortly after the *New York Times* announced Raskob's project, the stock market crash of 1929 threw the United States into a severe economic depression. Suddenly Raskob and his investors were strapped for cash. At the last minute, he was able to arrange a loan to save the $60 million project.

With the clock ticking away, Lamb worked feverishly to design the building. He revised one plan after another. Finally, on his fifteenth try, he came up with a simple plan that met all the city's zoning restrictions and Raskob's requirements. His finished product turned out to be far more majestic in appearance than Raskob had anticipated.

Lamb finished the basic design in four weeks. Scale models of the building filled his office as he worked on the details. Above his desk hung an artist's drawing of the finished building with the completion deadline of May 1, 1931, stamped in bold letters and figures.

There were numerous behind-the-scenes problems with designing a large building to such strict requirements. What was more important, well-lit

John Raskob asked his architect what style of building he had in mind. William Lamb reached across the desk and held up a sharpened pencil. This was the sort of simple, eye-pleasing design he hoped to build.

offices or spacious offices? Lamb opted for reducing the size of the rooms to 28 feet (8.5 meters) in depth, so they could all be built around the central core of elevators and service rooms, thus giving the offices the maximum in outside lighting.

What kind of elevator system could most efficiently transport people such great distances? Rather than use a single elevator, William Lamb broke up the elevator system into sections. The section serving the lower levels ended at mid-level where the building had to be set back; the upper elevators were placed in the central core. The Otis Elevator Company installed the 66 elevator cars.

How could you get water to the upper stories in the event of fire? Lamb designed a special fire-safety system with giant steel water tanks at six different levels, including one on the 101st floor. His system included 400 hose connections and a sprinkler system with an alarm connected to the city's central fire station. His design also specified the use of fireproof materials such as brick and limestone.

William Lamb completed the detailed final design within six months. Meanwhile, R. H. Shreve took responsibility for arranging the actual construction. Since the work would occur in the middle of one of the busiest cities in the world, storing building materials would be nearly impossible. Therefore, everything had to be put in place as it was delivered. For example, three days after factories in Pittsburgh formed a steel beam, construction workers were installing it in the building. Shreve had to arrange for tremendous quantities of all types of

The logic of the plan was simple. A certain amount of space in the center, arranged as compactly as possible, contains the vertical circulation, mail chutes, toilets, shafts, and corridors. Surrounding this is a perimeter of office space 28 feet deep. The sizes of the floors diminished as the elevators decrease in number. In essence there is a pyramid of non-rentable space surrounded by a greater pyramid of rentable space, a principle modified of course by practical considerations of construction and elevator operation.
—William Lamb,
The Architectural Forum, 1931

material—tons of marble from quarries in France and Italy for the main-floor lobby, 6,500 windows, 10 million bricks. He planned the project so carefully that he knew the exact number of rivets needed to fasten the steel beams together. Contractors would have a progress chart each day listing what each truck carried, where the material was to go, and who was responsible for it.

Just when everything seemed on track, Walter Chrysler dealt Raskob a stunning blow. Determined to have the world's tallest building, Chrysler had hidden his true plans for the Chrysler Building. After Lamb had designed the Empire State Building to be higher than the Chrysler Building, which was already under construction, Chrysler sprang the surprise. He had secretly constructed a spire inside the building. As the building reached completion, he opened the dome on top of his structure. Up came the spire that raised his building to 1,046 feet (319 meters), just a few feet higher than Lamb's design.

Chrysler's surprise threw Raskob and Lamb into a panic. Their plans were so far along that they could not afford to start over and redesign a building to beat Chrysler. But at an emergency brain-storming meeting, Raskob came up with an idea. "A hat!" he cried. "That's what this building needs—a hat!"

At Raskob's suggestion, Lamb added a 200-foot (61-meter) top, called a mooring mast, that would allow blimps to dock and discharge their passengers. The Goodyear Zeppelin officials, who operated a fleet of blimps, enthusiastically endorsed the idea. The mast proved to be impractical; it was

The distinctive spire of the Chrysler Building was clad in chrome-nickel steel, inspired by the automobile.

A **blimp** is a powered, steerable lighter-than-air craft called an airship. With its non- or semi-rigid frame, it looks like a long, giant balloon.

only used once. But it reclaimed for the Empire State Building the title of the world's tallest building.

Few experts believed that construction workers could complete the massive project in anything close to Raskob's ambitious deadline. But he put enormous pressure on everyone to finish the job on time. As construction began, one of Raskob's associates, former New York governor Al Smith, invited then New York governor Franklin D. Roosevelt to attend the building's opening, which was scheduled for May 1, 1931. Familiar with construction delays, Roosevelt guessed that the opening would probably take place the following October. "No, you put it down on the calendar," Smith insisted.

During the demolition of the Waldorf-Astoria Hotel, workers dug down to bedrock, 33 feet (10 meters) below the sidewalks. Then they began the most spectacular flurry of construction the world had ever seen. Work on the frame officially began on March 17, 1930. As many as 3,000 workers crawled over the growing steel skeleton like spiders on a web. Large cranes moved the steel girders into place, and gangs of riveters secured these girders by pounding red-hot rivets, or bolts, into place. Each gang had four workers. A heater kept a forge full of rivets that he tossed up to the catcher, who caught the fiery metal in a can. After the catcher placed the rivet into a hole in the steel plate, the bucker-up held it until the gunman smashed the rivet in with a riveting hammer.

In order to speed the materials to the right spot, the workers laid narrow-gauge railroad tracks

By May 1930, the framework for the Empire State Building had risen to the 12th floor.

up to and on each floor. Cars laden with metal parts, wire, lumber, or pipes were sent up the tracks to the floors where needed.

As spectators watched in fascination, the building shot up into the sky at a record rate. In one 10-day period, workers added 14 floors to the structure! Even the workers were astounded at how fast the building was going up. Yet the organization

Photographer Lewis Hine climbed to great heights to take his now-famous photographs of workers constructing the Empire State Building. These riveters had a great view of the rival Chrysler Building.

was so thorough and careful that, despite its location at 34th Street and Fifth Avenue—one of the busiest intersections in the world—construction work did not cause a single traffic jam or injury to a passerby. All building materials were received under the building and hoisted up to workers through the center. Five workers did lose their lives in various accidents, but the death rate was lower than on similar projects.

At the peak of construction, there were about 3,000 workers on the job at one time. Among them were 225 carpenters, 290 bricklayers, 384 brick laborers, 107 derrick men, 285 steel men, 249 elevator installers, 105 electricians, 192 plumbers, 194 heating and ventilating specialists, and various inspectors, checkers, foremen, clerks, and water carriers.

The steel frame was completed in six months, 23 days ahead of Lamb's ambitious schedule. One year and 45 days after laying the first piece of steel, the building was completed, easily within the deadline. Despite this pace, the contractors did not sacrifice quality. Shreve bragged that the building was within 5/8 of an inch (15 millimeters) of being perfectly vertical, and even in high winds it bends only 1/4 inch (6 millimeters) at the 85th floor. Because of the Great Depression, which had idled many workers and made them desperate for employment even at lower wages, the Empire State Building came in $2 million under budget.

There would be little work for the crew members after the completion of the building. The rate of new construction in New York City dropped 50 percent in the one year following the stock market crash in October 1929. "Instead of getting on line to sign up for the next job," wrote John Tauranac in *The Empire State Building*, "[these workmen] were in all likelihood going to stand on one line to sign up for relief, and then, when the benefits ran out, they would stand on another line—for bread."

Four and a half stories of steelwork were added each week. By June 20, twenty-six stories had been completed. On September 15, 1930, the steel was in place up to the eighty-sixth floor. A few days later, workmen standing 1,050 feet above the sidewalks of New York raised a large Stars and Stripes. . . . The builders of the Empire State Building threw steel into the sky not just higher but faster than anybody had ever dreamed possible.
—John Tauranac, author of *The Empire State Building*

THE RESULT

At the building's opening, on May 1, 1931—as scheduled—President Herbert Hoover turned on the lights from a switch in the White House. "Probably no building in the history of the world has brought about such universal interest in its progress," said Hoover. Al Smith's grandchildren cut the ribbon and Governor Franklin D. Roosevelt had indeed put the date on his calendar. He summed up the average person's reaction when he admitted, "I am a little awestruck. I have not got my sense of proportion back yet."

William Lamb, ironically, was not on hand to reap the praise for his efforts when the building was dedicated. He had sailed from New York to Europe the previous day. But R. H. Shreve made certain his partner received his due. Although many people helped to make the Empire State Building a reality, Shreve declared that the main credit for the building should go to Lamb, who designed it and who met the challenge of "the impossible demand for speed in construction."

William Lamb received the Architectural League's Medal of Honor in 1931. But when he died in 1952, he was relatively unheralded outside of his profession. Few people today have ever heard of him.

After the rush to finish construction, the building initially had trouble attracting enough tenants to make it profitable for its investors. During the Depression years, it was dubbed the "empty state building." Nonetheless, the Empire State Building immediately became—and remains—a symbol of New York City. Each year, millions of tourists ride up to its observation deck.

There were some doubts initially about the strength of the building. These were tragically erased on July 28, 1945, when a B-25 army bomber, its pilot apparently lost in the fog, slammed into the 79th floor of the building. Fourteen people died and 26 were injured. Despite the impact, the building stood firm and was repaired within three months.

The Empire State Building held the title of the world's tallest building for 40 years, until 1971 when the World Trade Center across town surpassed it. The Sears Tower in Chicago took the title just three years later at 1,454 feet (443 meters). The twin Petronas Towers in Kuala Lumpur, Malaysia, reached 1,476 feet (450 meters) when finished in 1996 and are now considered the tallest buildings in the world. The towers could lose this title when the Shanghai World Financial Center in China is completed in 2004. Plans for this building call for 94 stories that rise 1,509 feet (460 meters) from the ground.

But the Empire State Building, which in 1955 was honored by the American Society of Civil Engineers as one of the seven greatest engineering achievements in U.S. history, retains its place as the most famous and revered skyscraper ever built.

The Empire State Building rests on a five-story base. The first major setback is at the 6th floor, a second at the 30th floor. From there the building rises unbroken to the 80th floor. The building is faced with gray Bedford Indiana limestone, which contrasts nicely with the tomato-soup red window frames.

Modern Wonders
Built upon the Past

Today, engineering feats that would have astounded the world a half century ago are almost taken for granted. Recent record-holders do not inspire the same awe commanded by their predecessors. The 1,476-foot (450-meter) Petronas Towers constructed in Kuala Lumpur, Malaysia, in 1996 have attracted nowhere near the fame of the Empire State Building. Nor has the 1,824-foot (556-meter) CN Tower in Toronto, Canada, built in 1975, become a symbol rivaling the Eiffel Tower. Outside of Japan, few people have ever heard of the Akashi-Kaikyo Bridge, whose main span of 6,529 feet (1,900 meters) is four times longer than the Brooklyn Bridge.

One reason why tremendous building projects have slipped from legendary status is that mathematical calculations have overshadowed human personalities. In previous centuries, improvements in construction came about from trial and error as engineers and architects tested the limits of what

The twin Petronas Towers, designed by famous architect Cesar Pelli, are joined with a bridge at the 42nd story. The Malaysian oil company Petronas occupies the building.

had been done before. For the most part, this was a slow process—slow enough that individual innovations stood out and earned recognition. In recent years, project leaders have been able to test their ideas by running them through a computer program. In a fraction of a second, the computer can crank out calculations or refine plans on screen, far removed from public observation.

The Louisiana Superdome in New Orleans ranks as one of the most impressive and innovative pieces of modern engineering. Built in the early 1970s, its domed roof rises 273 feet (82 meters) from the ground and covers 9.7 acres (3.8 hectares), providing room for more than 75,000 people to comfortably watch a football game. During its construction, the builders had to rest the dome on 37 temporary towers. Each held a hydraulic jack so engineers could lower the entire dome onto a permanent supporting ring made of welded steel. Since the building is located in a hurricane zone, it also had to be designed to stand up to tremendous winds.

Individual credit for the Superdome, however, cannot be easily given. The facility was a collaborative effort. Many unnamed individuals contributed to the development of the improved construction materials used in the dome, such as reinforced and prestressed concrete and high-strength steel.

Similarly, construction of the English Channel Tunnel (known as the "Chunnel" for short) was a mind-boggling feat of engineering. After more than 200 years of preposterous schemes and false starts, work on the present tunnel began in December

The Louisiana Superdome has hosted five Super Bowls, more than any other facility. It holds the world record for attendance at an indoor concert—87,500 fans heard the Rolling Stones play there in 1981.

1987. Financiers poured more than $13 billion into the project (an average of $4.5 million per day). By the mid-1990s, engineers and construction workers had carved out three parallel tunnels, 31 miles (50 kilometers) long, through the chalky ground beneath the English Channel. One of these is a utility tunnel and the other two carry trains. Again, no one person's name is stamped on the planning and supervision of the greatest tunnel in the world. Hundreds of engineers joined to accomplish the goal.

If individual engineers and architects of the future are to recapture people's imaginations, they will probably have to take the route of Richard Buckminster Fuller. Born in Milton, Massachusetts, in 1895, young Bucky Fuller saw the world as nothing but a blur of different shapes until the age of four. Although glasses corrected his vision problem, he never forgot how he had once viewed the world.

Bucky Fuller's unique understanding of shapes led to a breakthrough. In the late 1940s, it occurred to him that a dome was the most logical structure for a building. After all, it was half of a sphere, a shape that enclosed the most space with the least surface area. Then Fuller found he could draw circles on the surface of the sphere in such a way that the entire surface was divided into triangles.

Fuller knew that the triangle was the strongest, most stable shape. A sphere made of connecting triangles, then, should have the combined qualities of a sphere and a triangle, and a dome, or half-sphere, should be the strongest and most economical form for building. Fuller experimented with these

R. Buckminster Fuller received a patent for the geodesic dome on June 29, 1954. His most impressive structure was a huge sphere, 250 feet (80 meters) in diameter, that he designed for the 1967 World's Fair in Montreal, Canada.

triangle-based, or "geodesic" domes. Before long, he had created very lightweight domes that could support tremendously heavy weights.

Fuller's geodesic dome is probably the most innovative construction idea to appear in the past half century. He suggested bold ideas for it, such as a dome over Manhattan Island that would make it 50 times more energy efficient. But, so far, no one has made use of the geodesic dome to produce the kind of colossal structure that would rival those presented in this book.

Someday, however, perhaps in the near future, a person may appear who can combine some of the genius of Fuller, Imhotep, and Brunel with the innovative tinkering of Roebling, Eiffel, and Crowe; the practical expertise of Lamb; and the organizational mastery of Goethals. If that happens, the result will be something that will enchant our world as these creative engineering geniuses amazed theirs.

TALLEST BUILDINGS

1.	Petronas Tower 1	Kuala Lumpur, Malaysia	1996	1,476 ft[†]	450 m
2.	Petronas Tower 2	Kuala Lumpur, Malaysia	1996	1,476 ft	450 m
3.	Sears Tower	Chicago, Ill., USA	1974	1,454 ft	443 m
4.	Jin Mao Building	Shanghai, China	1998	1,379 ft	420 m
5.	1 World Trade Center	New York, N.Y., USA	1972	1,368 ft	417 m
6.	2 World Trade Center	New York, N.Y., USA	1973	1,362 ft	415 m
7.	Empire State Building	New York, N.Y., USA	1931	1,250 ft	381 m
8.	Central Plaza	Hong Kong, China	1992	1,227 ft	374 m
9.	Bank of China Tower	Hong Kong, China	1989	1,209 ft	369 m
10.	T & C Tower	Kaoshiung, Taiwan	1997	1,140 ft	347 m
11.	Amoco	Chicago, Ill., USA	1973	1,136 ft	346 m
12.	John Hancock Center	Chicago, Ill., USA	1969	1,127 ft	344 m

[†]Height is measured from sidewalk level to the structural top of the building. Antennas and flagpoles are not included.

LONGEST BRIDGES

1.	Akashi Kaikyo	Awaji Island-Kobe, Japan	1998	6,529 ft[*]	1,990 m
2.	Store Bælt	Sjaelland-Fyn Islands, Denmark	1998	5,328 ft	1,624 m
3.	Humber	Hull, England	1981	4,626 ft	1,410 m
4.	Tsing Ma	Hong Kong, China	1997	4,518 ft	1,377 m
5.	Verrazano-Narrows	New York, N.Y., USA	1964	4,260 ft	1,298 m
6.	Golden Gate	San Francisco Bay, Calif., USA	1937	4,200 ft	1,280 m
7.	Mackinac	Sts. of Mackinac, Mich., USA	1957	3,800 ft	1,158 m
8.	Minami Bisan-Seto	Shikoku-Honshu Islands, Japan	1988	3,609 ft	1,100 m
9.	Bosphorus	Istanbul, Turkey	1973	3,524 ft	1,074 m
10.	George Washington	New York, N.Y., USA	1931	3,500 ft	1,067 m
11.	Ponte 25 de Abril	Lisbon, Portugal	1966	3,323 ft	1,013 m
12.	Bosphorus II	Istanbul, Turkey	1988	3,322 ft	1,012 m

[*]Length is determined by the longest span. A span is the distance between a bridge's supports.

GLOSSARY

agitator: a tool or machine that shakes or stirs a substance

alloy: A mixture of one metal with another, such as brass, which is an alloy of copper and zinc, or a mix of one metal with a nonmetal, such as steel, which is an alloy of iron combined with small amounts of carbon and other substances. Alloys are useful because their characteristics are often quite different from the pure metals from which they are made. Based on a Latin word "to bind."

arch: a structure shaped like an upside-down U. The upper edge can be curved, pointed, or flat, and it usually supports the weight above it, as in a doorway.

arch bridge: a roadway supported by an arch or series of arches, often made of brick or stone

architect: a person who designs and supervises the construction of buildings and other structures

bedrock: the solid rock of the Earth's crust that usually lies under layers of topsoil, sand, and small rocks

bends, the: a painful condition caused by a change in water pressure. When underwater, the pressure begins to dissolve nitrogen gas in a person's blood. If this pressure is suddenly relieved, the nitrogen again becomes gas and can form bubbles that block oxygen in the blood stream. This lack of oxygen to body parts causes the bends.

blimp: a powered, steerable lighter-than-air craft called an airship. With its non- or semi-rigid frame, it looks like a long, giant balloon.

bore: to form a tunnel or hole by drilling or digging

boring: the interior diameter of a hole, tube, or tunnel

bridge: a structure that extends over and provides a way across a gap or barrier such as a river

caisson: a watertight device used in construction that allows projects to be built underwater. French word meaning "large box."

canal: a waterway built to join two or more bodies of water

canyon: a narrow opening between steep cliff walls

carbon: a common, nonmetallic chemical element found in all plants and animals. Coal, charcoal, graphite, and diamonds are different forms of carbon.

carbon monoxide: a deadly poisonous gas that has no odor or color and is produced when a substance containing carbon does not have enough oxygen to burn completely. For example, carbon monoxide can be emitted by poorly ventilated furnaces or by gasoline-powered engines.

caulking: a material used to seal or fill seams and cracks to make something airtight or watertight. For example, the seams of a wooden ship are filled with tar or pitch.

cement: a gray powder made from crushed limestone and clay. Mixed with water, pebbles, and sand, it hardens into a stonelike construction material called concrete.

civil engineer: an engineer trained in the design and construction of large public works such as roads, bridges, dams, sewers, or canals

concrete: a building material made from cement, sand, pebbles, and water. When soft, concrete can be shaped. It dries into a hard, rocklike substance. **Reinforced concrete** has metal rods added for strength. From the Latin word meaning "to become solid."

culvert: a sewer or drainpipe that crosses under a road or embankment

dam: a wall or barrier built across a river to control the flow of water. Water held back can be used for drinking, irrigation, or to power electric plants. Dams can be made of earth and rock or of concrete.

dehydration: to remove water from a substance. Medically, excessive loss of water from a person's body.

drainage basin: the area of land from which small streams and rainfall drain, or flow, into a river system

dredge: to deepen harbors and waterways with a machine or boat equipped with scooping or suction devices

excavation: a hole formed by excavating, or digging

geodesic dome: a half-sphere structure made up of interlocking triangles

girder: a horizontal beam made of metal or wood used as a main support for a bridge or building

hemp: a plant, the fibers of which are used to make strong rope or coarse cloth

hydraulic: having to do with water or liquids; also describes a machine that runs on the pressure of water or liquids

iron: a hard, silver-gray metallic element that is strongly magnetic and is the most common metal on Earth. Iron ores are refined in a blast furnace to produce blocks called pig iron, which can be remelted and poured into molds to make **cast iron**, or commercially purified to make **wrought iron**, or alloyed with carbon and other elements to make **steel**.

jumbo: a huge motorized rig equipped with 30 rock drills used in tunneling during construction of the Hoover Dam. The miners rode the rig, drilled, filled the holes with dynamite, then backed out of the tunnel and blasted. After workers removed the debris, the jumbos moved back in the tunnel to repeat the process.

limestone: a sedimentary rock made up mostly of the mineral calcite; often used in buildings and in the steel and chemical industries

lock: a section of a waterway enclosed by gates in which boats are raised or lowered by raising or lowering the water level

mastaba: a large, low-built rectangular tomb constructed with bricks made of mud and straw. The burial chamber was dug deep into the ground beneath the mastaba.

mausoleum: a large stately building housing one or several burial vaults

metallurgy: the science and technology of metals, including mining and refining metals from their ores, making alloys, and shaping metals. A scientist who studies metals is called a **metallurgist.**

necropolis: a large and elaborate cemetery. From the Greek words *necro,* which means dead body or corpse, and *polis,* which means city.

pneumatic: containing air or functioning by using air

Ptah: ancient Egyptian god of arts and crafts

pyramid: a huge monument of ancient Egypt that was built over a tomb and has a rectangular base with four triangular sides that meet at the top

quicksand: loose sand and water forming a soft mass that tends to engulf any object on its surface

rivet: a metal bolt with a head on one end inserted through aligned holes in the pieces to be joined and then hammered on the plain end to form a second head

skyscraper: a modern building of great height constructed on a steel skeleton with elevators to transport people from floor to floor. Early skyscrapers were about 10 stories tall; later ones rose 100 stories or more.

steel: a metal alloy of iron with small amounts of carbon and traces of other elements

subaqueous: made or adapted for underwater use. In Latin, *sub* means under and *aqua* means water.

suspension bridge: a bridge with the roadway suspended from cables that are anchored at each end and often supported by towers

ventilation: the process of circulating fresh air into a building or other place. Vent comes from a Latin word meaning "wind."

BIBLIOGRAPHY

Berton, Pierre. *Niagara: A History of the Falls.* New York: Kodansha America, 1992.

Bishop, Joseph Bucklin. *Goethals: Genius of the Panama Canal.* New York: Harper, 1930.

Bobrick, Benson. *Labyrinths of Iron.* New York: Newsweek Books, 1981.

Boring, Mel. *Incredible Constructions and the People Who Built Them.* New York: Walker, 1984.

Brown, David J. *The Random House Book of How Things Were Built.* New York: Random House, 1992.

Cameron, Ian. *The Impossible Dream.* New York: Morrow, 1972.

Carroll, David. *The Taj Mahal: India Under the Moguls.* New York: Newsweek Books, 1972.

Chafin, Andrew. *Louisiana Superdome.* Louisiana Stadium Commission, 1975.

Corbett, Scott. *Bridges.* New York: Four Winds, 1978.

Davidovits, Joseph, and Margie Morris. *The Pyramids: An Enigma Solved.* New York: Hippocrene, 1988.

Dunar, Andrew J., and Dennis McBride. *Building Hoover Dam: An Oral History of the Great Depression.* New York: Macmillan, 1993.

DuVal, Miles P., Jr. *And the Mountains Will Move: The Story of the Building of the Panama Canal.* New York: Greenwood Press, 1968.

Edwards, I. E. S. *The Pyramids of Egypt.* London: Penguin, 1993.

"Empire State Tower, Tallest In World, Is Opened by Hoover." *New York Times,* May 2, 1931.

Evans, G. Russell. *The Panama Canal Treaties Swindle: Consent to Disaster.* Carrboro, N.C.: Signal Books, 1986.

Fakhry, Ahmed. *The Pyramids.* Chicago: University of Chicago Press, 1961.

Gies, Joseph. *Bridges and Men.* New York: Doubleday, 1963.

Harriss, Joseph. "A Parisian Love Affair." *Reader's Digest,* March 1989, pp. 57-62.

———. *The Tallest Tower: Eiffel and the Belle Epoque.* Washington, D.C.: Regnery Gateway, 1975.

Hawass, Zahi A. *The Pyramids of Ancient Egypt.* Pittsburgh: Carnegie Museum of Natural History, 1990.

Jacobs, David, and Anthony Neville. *Bridges, Canals and Tunnels.* New York: American Heritage, 1968.

Keller, Ulrich. *The Building of the Panama Canal in Historic Photographs.* New York: Dover, 1983.

LaFeber, Walter. *The Panama Canal: The Crisis in Historical Perspective.* New York: Oxford University Press, 1978.

Lehner, Mark. *The Complete Pyramids.* New York: Thames and Hudson, 1997.

Loyrette, Henri. *Gustave Eiffel*. New York: Rizzoli, 1985.

McCullough, David G. *The Great Bridge: the Epic Story of the Building of the Brooklyn Bridge*. New York: Simon and Schuster, 1972.

————. *The Path Between the Seas: the Creation of the Panama Canal, 1870-1914*. New York: Simon and Schuster, 1977.

Mack, Gerstle. *The Land Divided*. New York: Knopf, 1944.

McNeese, Tim. *The Panama Canal*. San Diego: Lucent, 1997.

Mann, Elizabeth. *The Brooklyn Bridge*. New York: Mikaya Press, 1996.

Navailles, Jean-Pierre. "Eiffel's Tower." *History Today*, December 1989.

Olney, Ross R. *They Said It Couldn't Be Done*. New York: Dutton, 1979.

O'Neal, Michael. *Pyramids: Opposing Viewpoints*. San Diego: Greenhaven, 1995.

Parker, Nancy Winslow. *Locks, Crocks, and Skeeters: The Story of the Panama Canal*. New York: Greenwillow, 1996.

Potter, Robert. *R. Buckminster Fuller*. Englewood Cliffs, N.J.: Silver Burdett, 1990.

The Pyramids and Sphinx. New York: Newsweek Books, 1971.

Robertson, Donald W. *Mind's Eye of Buckminster Fuller*. New York: Vantage, 1974.

St. George, Judith. *The Brooklyn Bridge: They Said It Couldn't Be Built*. New York: G. P. Putnam's Sons, 1982.

————. *Panama Canal: Gateway to the World*. New York: G. P. Putnam's Sons, 1989.

Smith, Carter, III. *The Pyramid Builders*. Englewood Cliffs, N.J.: Silver Burdett, 1991.

Steinman, David B., and Sara Ruth Watson. *Bridges and Their Builders*. New York: Putnam, 1941.

Stevens, Joseph E. *The Hoover Dam: An American Adventure*. Norman: University of Oklahoma Press, 1988.

Taubes, Gary. "Twinkle, Twinkle, Great Big Bauble." *Discover*, November 1987, pp. 60-64.

Tauranac, John. *The Empire State Building: The Making of a Landmark*. New York: Scribner, 1995.

Watson, Philip. *Egyptian Pyramids and Mastaba Tombs*. Aylesbury, U.K.: Shire, 1987.

Weingarten, Arthur. *The Sky Is Falling*. New York: Grosset and Dunlap, 1977.

ABOUT THE AUTHOR

Nathan Aaseng is an award-winning author of over 100 fiction and nonfiction books for young readers. He writes on subjects ranging from science and technology to business, government, politics, and law. Aaseng's books for The Oliver Press include the *Business Builders* series and nine titles in the *Great Decisions* series. He lives with his wife, Linda, and their four children in Eau Claire, Wisconsin.

PHOTO ACKNOWLEDGMENTS

AP/Wide World Photos: p. 116

Archive Photos: cover, pp. 9, 19, 42 (top left), 49 (bottom), 69, 72, 91, 114, 128

Avery Architectural and Fine Arts Library, Columbia University: pp. 118, 123, 124

Corbiss Bettmann Archive: pp. 12 (bottom), 14, 73 (all), 74

Dictionary of American Portraits: pp. 99 (Library of Congress), 115 (both, top engraving by H. B. Hall's Sons)

Don Berliner: p. 132

Empire State Building, managed by Helmsley-Spear, Inc.: p. 127

Frank Leslie's Illustrated News: p. 11 (top)

Guildhall Library, Corporation of London: pp. 26 (bottom), 33, 34, 37, 40-41

Harper's New Monthly Magazine: p. 56

Harper's Weekly: pp. 53, 54

Library of Congress: pp. 2, 6, 11 (bottom), 12 (top), 23, 25, 26 (top), 29, 30, 42 (bottom), 62 (both), 67, 75, 76 (bottom), 78, 81 (both), 82, 87, 89, 94 (top), 97, 112 (top), 117, 121

Museum of the City of New York: pp. 52, 57, 61

National Archives: p. 76 (top)

National Portrait Gallery, London: p. 39

Nevada Historical Society: pp. 100, 102, 104, 108, 111, back cover

Nevada State Museum and Historical Society: p. 94 (bottom)

New York Times **News Service:** p. 112 (bottom)

Revilo: pp. 45, 79, 85

Roebling Collection, Institute of Archives and Special Collections, Rensselaer Polytechnic Institute, Troy, New York: pp. 42 (top right), 49 (top)

Scientific American: pp. 47, 50, 58